C.G. Hussey

Copper, Steel, & Philanthropy in 19th century Pittsburgh

Christopher C. Binns

eBook ISBN: 978-1-966931-07-2
Paperback ISBN: 978-1-966931-08-9
Hardback ISBN: 978-1-966931-09-6

Table of Contents

Foreword

When Dr. Curtis Grubb Hussey died in 1893 in Pittsburgh, at the age of 90 he had not only covered most of the 19th-century chronologically but also had exemplified a protean American paradigm of that century. C. G. Hussey was a frontier physician, owner of a chain of western stores, wholesale pork trader, copper and steel magnate, inventor, banker, and a philanthropist who supported a broad range of that era's educational, scientific, and progressive causes.

Hussey appears in many accounts of the growth of industrial Pittsburgh but is typically not as central to the story. This may be explained, ironically, by the seniority of his contributions to industrialization, particularly with respect to steel. Even the greatest steel magnate of all, Andrew Carnegie, acknowledged Hussey as an early influence in his autobiography.[2] However, Hussey's major contributions were at the onset of the American copper and steel industries, well before the explosion of steel manufacturing which defined the era of the Robber Barons and the Gilded Age of the late 19th-century. In addition, Hussey did not leave a strong paper trail: no autobiography, no trove of personal papers. He was reputed to be modest and socially retiring according to some of the somewhat hagiographic short biographies written while he still lived.

Perhaps he preferred this low profile and managed it as cannily as he managed his professional and philanthropic interests. Or perhaps he simply was as modest as he was reputed to have been. For a man who was at one time reputed to be the richest man in Pittsburgh and who was essentially the founder of the modern copper and steel industries in America, Hussey has a remarkably low profile in history. With no evidence of the existence of Hussey's personal papers or correspondence, this short biography views Hussey through the lens of the businesses and institutions with which he was associated. Therefore, in recounting his story, I have offered summaries of technical detail, such as mining or smelting technology, as well as social trends, including the education of women and African- Americans. Others have covered all these areas in far greater detail, but some understanding of these industries and institutions in the mid-19th-century is critical to capturing a picture of this seminal character, however indistinctly.

I came to Hussey a few years ago through a genealogical chart that has always been in my family, and which was apparently compiled by my paternal great-grandfather, Ralph Holden Binns, around 1900. In family lore, R. H. Binns was the font of fabulous wealth, which he lost just after World War I, recouped somewhat in the 1920s, then lost for good in the Great Depression.

According to this narrative, we have marched inexorably through four generations of downward economic mobility. One day, Googling names a bit upstream on the genealogical chart, I ran across an excerpt of a short 19th-century biography of C. G. Hussey, posted in the family genealogical blog of Duncan Rea Williams.

This biography, published in the *Magazine of Western History* in 1886, while Hussey was still alive, quickly made it clear that our family had misjudged by two generations the economic heights from which it had fallen. The real source of the lost wealth was Hussey, the grandfather of Ralph Holden Binns. From this start, I found other short contemporary accounts in biographical encyclopedias that proliferated in the late 19th-century.

Like the first one I had read, they were unsourced, seemed excessively fawning and tended to repeat each other, suggesting that they all came from the same source, the 1886 *Magazine of Western History* article. Intrigued, I began to track Hussey's story down in other accounts of the history of the copper and steel industry and in accounts of the many institutions affected by his philanthropy, which were broad but tended to focus on educational advancement, particularly for women and African Americans. I assumed his life would only be of interest to us, his family. But the more threads I followed, the more I came to believe that Curtis Hussey's life is worthy of broader exposure, if only for the astonishing breadth of his interests. In commerce, he was often present at the inception not only of a business but of whole industries that came to define the burgeoning economic power of late 19th-century America. Similarly, in philanthropy, he was often on the cutting edge of new institutions that radically supported social justice or educational and scientific advancement in ways that still feel modern today.

Christopher C. Binns
Dorchester 2017

Tryouts

Curtis Grubb Hussey made his name and fortune in copper and steel in the early days of those industries in Pittsburgh in the 1840s and 1850s. But before he settled in Pittsburgh in 1840, he had already prospered in several ventures farther west in the frontier states of Ohio and Indiana.

Born August 11, 1802, in York, Pennsylvania, to Christopher Hussey and Lydia Grubb Hussey, C.G. Hussey moved with his family to Little Miami, Ohio, then in 1813 to Mt. Pleasant, Ohio. An earlier Christopher Hussey had been a representative to the General Court (legislature) of Massachusetts in the 1600s and had been part of a group of Quakers who bought land from the Native Americans on Nantucket in 1658-59 to escape Puritan persecution.[3]

The Husseys of Mt. Pleasant, like their founding member in America, were devout Quakers, and the small village of Mt. Pleasant was the Midwest epicenter for the Society of Friends. In 1814, The Quakers built an immense meetinghouse in the village, which served as the annual meeting place for the whole Midwest.

As befit the socially conscious Quaker denomination, Mt. Pleasant was a hotbed of antislavery activity, likely fed by its proximity to the substantial slave mart of Wheeling, Virginia (now West Virginia). Mt. Pleasant was a well-documented and critical first stop on the Underground Railway, with many known hiding spots. In 1817, the Quaker Charles Osborn established *The Philanthropist,* the first newspaper in the country advocating the abolition of slavery, in Mount Pleasant.[4] In 1821, the Quaker abolitionist Benjamin Lundy started publishing *The Genius of Universal Emancipation*, another abolitionist newspaper, also in Mount Pleasant.[5] Activists in the village created a free school for Black children and opened a Free Labor Store in 1848.[6] Free Labor Stores aimed never to buy or sell anything that was tainted by the use of slave labor. The Mt. Pleasant Free Labor Store closed in 1857, which speaks less to the commitment of the villagers to their antislavery sentiments than to the near impossibility of economic activity not tainted by the tentacles of slavery.

Perhaps the Husseys moved to Mt. Pleasant because of the compatibility of their religious and political beliefs with those of their Quaker brethren, or perhaps their beliefs were shaped by their lives there, but Curtis Grubb Hussey was deeply entwined with the people, politics, and religion of Mt. Pleasant. Jonathan Binns, the man who later became his brother-in-law by marrying his sister, Elizabeth McPherson Hussey, was a banker and the director of the Free Labor Board. The Binns house on the edge of town was believed to have been a stop on the underground railway, being described as:

> ... at a high elevation and several stories high with widow's walk on the roof on which they reportedly placed a lamp at night. Slaves escaping from the Virginia Slave Auctions near Martin's Ferry and Wheeling were told to follow the light

north to freedom. The house also had a single- story kitchen in the back with the roof joining just below a back window that was out of sight. When the present owner began extending the room the workers removed a large vent-like structure on this roof to find that it was a trap door leading to a hiding place in the rafters. Inside the rafters was found an ancient coat probably belonging to an escaping slave.[7]

While in Mt. Pleasant, Hussey trained as a physician, beginning in 1820. He lived only a dozen years in Mt. Pleasant, moving west in 1825. The profession he trained for there did not turn out to be his life's work. Yet throughout his life he remained involved not only with relatives in the village but with the causes that were deeply rooted in the 19th-century Quaker social justice outlook, causes which were woven deeply into the Mt. Pleasant society of his youth.

In 1825 Hussey left Mt. Pleasant, Ohio, and moved to Mooresville in Morgan County, Indiana, to set up his medical practice. This was the West in Hussey's time. Both Ohio and Indiana were carved out of the Northwest Territory, Ohio in 1803 and Indiana in 1816, the Northwest Territory being that part of the United States ceded from Britain but not part of the original thirteen states. Not until the Louisiana Purchase of 1805 were the lands beyond the Mississippi even part of the United States. Hussey was literally a physical pioneer, born and raised in the West, and moving to the most remote part of it in Indiana as a young man. While his serial entrepreneurial efforts eventually took him back to Pittsburgh, that city was essentially the capital of "the West" and his later industrial ventures often showed evidence of a Western outlook not always in tune with Eastern industrialists who, at first glance, might have seemed more likely allies.

If Indiana was the frontier, Morgan County and Mooresville in south-central Indiana were the edges of that frontier when Hussey arrived. While Hussey may have selected Morgan County because it was settled primarily by Quakers who had fled the South, it had only been founded in 1822.[8]

Mooresville itself was first settled in 1819, and Hussey's house was among the first five houses in Mooresville.[9] Within four years of setting up his practice in Indiana, Hussey had purchased a local general store. He acquired several other stores in the next few years in Gosport, Monrovia, Columbus, Millvale, and Far West; for example, in 1834 he and two partners purchased a store in neighboring Monrovia that held stock worth $2000,[10] a substantial shop inventory anywhere in the 1830s, let along in an Indiana frontier town. His string of general stores led to his next business venture: pigs. Having accepted in-kind payments, especially pigs, in both his medical work and his stores, but not finding enough local market for pork, he set up a pork processing plant in Gosport, Indiana and began shipping pork downriver to New Orleans and to the East through Pittsburgh.[11]

Throughout his life Hussey always adhered to and supported the social- justice stances of 19th-century Quakerism, but he may have been less enamored of the strict observance of Quaker mores, at least as a young man. Modern Friends practice a very gentle and open-minded religious observance, in addition to supporting social justice. Nineteenth-century Friends, like even the most liberal Christians of the time, were devout in a way more associated today with evangelical Christians. Quakers were prolific publishers of religious tracts, and these 19th-century publications display the significance believers placed in a personal relationship with an active and demanding God who guided them daily in all their actions and thoughts and in the importance of adhering to a strict moral and religious code, however communally these might be enforced. Early in his tenure in Indiana, Hussey ran afoul of those codes. He joined the local Friends meeting in Short Creek, Indiana, on January 22, 1828, as reported by the minutes of the monthly White Lick meeting in May of that year.[12] However, on July 7,1830, the monthly White Lick meeting reported that:

> White Lick Preparative complains of Curtis G. Hussey for neglecting the attendance of our meetings, dividing from plain dress and address, and for attending a marriage contrary to discipline. Samuel Owen, and Edward Chammess [?] are appointed to visit him on the occasion and to [report to the] next meeting.[13]

These complaints are typical in meeting minutes and are usually immediately complied with, as reported in the following month's meeting. They also usually only refer to one issue, such as attending a wedding out of the Friends, not a litany such as was directed at Hussey. The remonstrance with Hussey did not go well at first, as reported the following month:

> Those appointed last month to visit Curtis G. Hussey report they had an opportunity with him to but little satisfaction, they have produced a testification against him which was approved and signed. Edward Bray and John Carter Junior are appointed to offer him a copy thereof, inform him of his right of appeal and report next meeting.[14]

That was enough for Hussey. He buckled and the appointed men reported back at the following meeting that he had complied with the demands of the Meeting.[15]

While most of his career centered on copper and steel, Hussey maintained a hand in pork produce long past when it was the center of his business, although this may have been more related to the support of his extended family than because of a continuing personal interest in that business. For example, in 1865 his nephew A.H. Hussey, of the pork produce firm of Hussey, Goss & Co. of Gosport, reported paying C.G. Hussey $6259.69 as his share of the pork operations for 1864-1865:

Pork Sales Report from A.H. Hussey to C.G. Hussey, 1865[16]

Throughout his life, Hussey employed relatives like this, typically in geographically distant and commercially ancillary operations.

As his final act in Indiana, Hussey served one term in the Indiana legislature, in 1829-1830, then either retired or lost and lost again in a state senate race in 1833 as a member of the "Anti-Jackson" and Whig party.[17] While some of the contemporary short biographies mention the lower house term and say that he did not seek re-election because he was more interested in tending to business, the fact that he later ran for the state senate suggests he may not yet have given up political ambition. However, throughout his many decades in Pittsburgh, he appears not to have engaged actively in politics, although he was always known as a strong Republican after the founding of that party in the 1850s.

The Republican positions opposing slavery and supporting high tariffs would dovetail neatly with the interests of not only Hussey, but also his fellow Pittsburgh industrialists. In fact, Hussey's main partner in both his later copper and steel ventures, Thomas Marshall Howe, had served as a Whig in Congress in the 1850s and remained a prominent and active Republican politician throughout his life.

With the assets he had accumulated from his pork trading business, Hussey returned to Mt. Pleasant in 1839 to marry Rebecca Updegraff, a member of a prominent local family. They promptly moved to Pittsburgh to better manage the expanding pork supply business from that trading and manufacturing hub. In Pittsburgh, he founded Hussey & Wells Co. pork packers in 1845, bringing into the business a young man named Calvin Wells, who remained a key Hussey associate for decades.

When he moved to Pittsburgh, Hussey may have just thought it was a better location from which to manage his pork distribution. Or, he may have considered that his restless entrepreneurial spirit would find wider scope in the metropolis and planned to leap to yet another level from the springboard of his success with pork, as he had from medicine to store ownership to pork. In any case, pork was not to remain the center of his business attention. Another pork business founded by Hussey with William B. Hays in 1850 was in Hays's name alone by no later than 1853.[18] While Hussey & Wells started out as a pork business, Wells eventually followed Hussey into the steel business as Hussey & Wells morphed from pork to steel in the late 1850s.

These changes were a decade and more beyond Hussey's arrival in Pittsburgh, but by the early 1840s he was already in a position to try something new. He took a chance and struck it big in a new field: copper.

Copper

In the 1840s, the American copper industry was crude: crudely mined, crudely refined, crudely marketed. C. G. Hussey changed all that in a mere five years. In 1845, he opened the first great copper mine in the Western hemisphere in the wilderness of Michigan's upper peninsula.

By 1849, he had invented and put into production copper smelting furnaces that became the standard for the next century. The following year he began marketing the products resulting from this purer and cheaper copper. By 1850 he was not only the technological leader and founder of the modern copper industry, but he also controlled a vertical slice of that industry.

Pittsburgh and Boston Mining Corporation and the Cliff mine

Hussey had moved to Pittsburgh in 1840 and was running his pork trading business from there when he met John Hays. Hays was a druggist, and they may have met through their allied professions, although it does not appear that Hussey was a practicing physician in Pittsburgh. In 1843 Hays had caught wind of possible copper deposits on Lake Superior's Keweenaw Peninsula in upper Michigan. He approached Hussey with that news.[19] Hays apparently complained to Hussey about his health and Hussey advised Hays to take a break from his druggist work and act on his taste for adventure by going to Michigan as Hussey's agent[20], which seems an odd bit of advice considering the difficulty and danger of the proposed trip into the wilderness. Hussey staked Hays's trip to Copper Harbor, Michigan in July 1843 to investigate, agreeing to pay half of Hays's expenses and to provide funds for mining leases.[21]

The following map of the Great Lakes shows the scope of the trip from Pittsburgh on the lower right to Hays' destination: Copper Harbor on the Keweenaw Peninsula, jutting out into Lake Superior on the upper left, with key stops from the trip indicated:

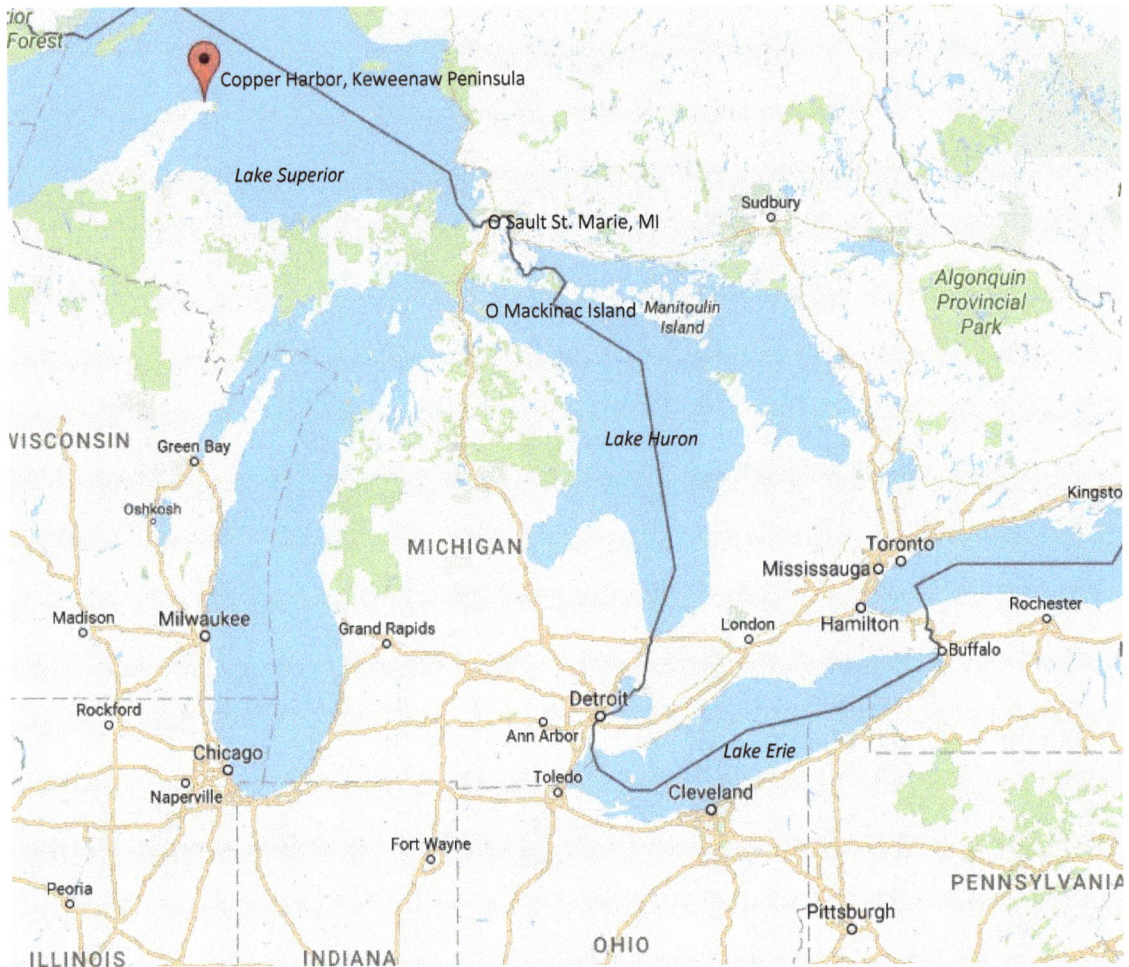

Great Lakes region, through which John Hays traveled to for Hussey[22]

The trip was arduous, over 1000 miles overland from Pittsburgh to Cleveland, then by boat the rest of the way. Hays left Pennsylvania and traveled by the steamer *Chesapeake* from Cleveland west across Lake Erie and north over Lake Huron to Mackinac Island, from which he set out for Lake Superior. Making his way still farther north, he traveled upriver past the rapids on St. Mary's River by canoe to Sault St. Marie, then by the schooner *Algonquin* to the port of Copper Harbor on the Keweenaw Peninsula.[23] As evidence of how primitive transportation was on Lake Superior, the *Algonquin* had been hauled by portage up to Sault St. Marie only in 1839, and beginning in 1840, was the first boat of any size larger than a traditional "bateau" to be hauled up past the rapids.[24] Anything larger than the bateaux had come from Canada to the north.

The following map shows Copper Harbor at the tip of the Keweenaw Peninsula, in Lake Superior, as well as the names of the major early mines. The Cliff Mine, the mine that made Hussey's first fortune, is the northernmost listed. The dotted line indicates the principal underlying copper deposits. The inset identifies the peninsula by the informal name which soon came to apply, Copper Country:

10

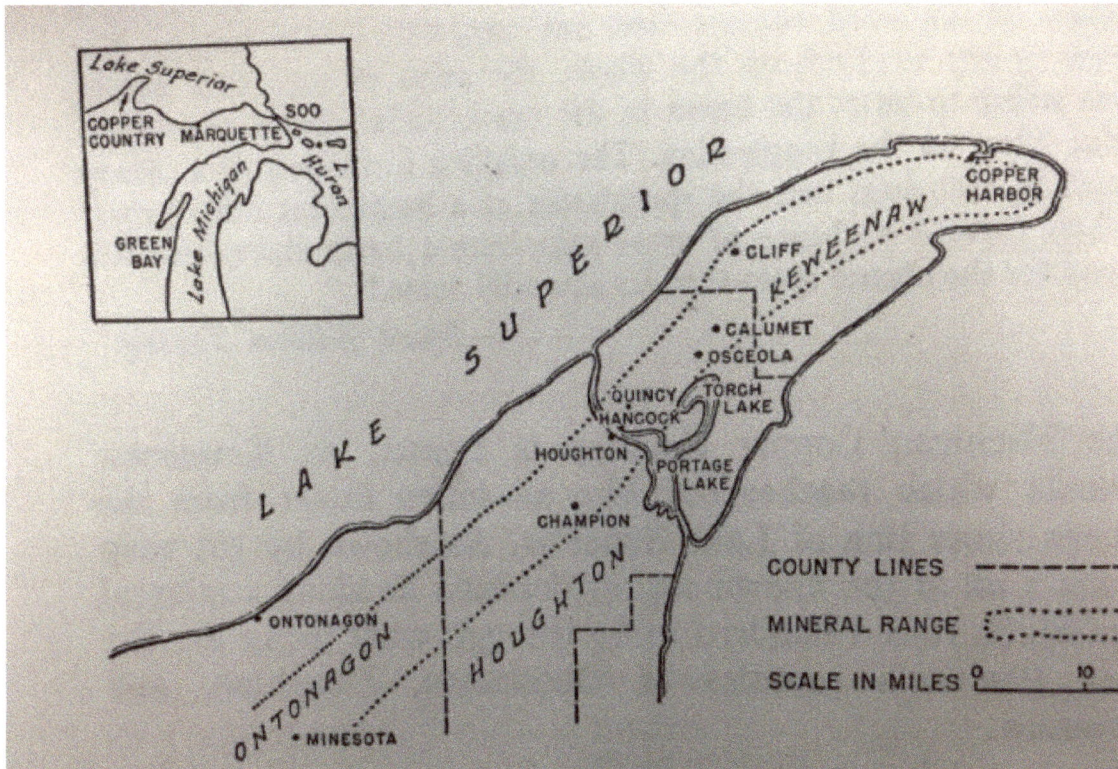

The Keeweenaw Peninsula and the early copper mines.[25]

Hays arrived at an opportune moment. In 1840, a survey by Douglass Houghton, later the first state geologist of Michigan, found potential for copper mining in the area.[26] The Treaty of LaPointe with Chippewa Indians went into effect in 1843, ceding 25,000 square miles to the United States, and the Federal Mineral Land Agency arrived at Copper Harbor on June 18, 1843, to manage the claims.[27]

Meanwhile, publicity about the mineral potential gained popular attention with the saga of the Ontonagon boulder. This enormous chunk of pure copper (3700 pounds, roughly four feet by three feet[28]) was purchased from the Chippewa Indians in 1841 and, in the summer of 1842, hauled overland to the Ontonagon River, then in the fall of 1843, shipped through Detroit to Buffalo for display, eventually arriving at the Smithsonian in Washington.[29]

The survey, the treaty and the other events of 1842-1843 events were likely the source of the information Hays shared with Hussey.

While there is some evidence that centuries before, the native peoples had mined copper for weapons and ornaments, in recent centuries the Indians had considered the copper sacred and did not use it. In the late 17th-century and early 18th-century several French mining attempts had failed and several British exploratory efforts succeeded the French.[30]

The demand for copper grew rapidly in the early 19th-century. In addition to its

11

traditional use in household goods such as pots and pans, and in decorative uses, copper sheathing had been found to protect ship bottoms from rotting and was in great demand as navies expanded.

Then, as steam power grew, copper was prized for the manufacture of boilers and wire. From a total world copper production of 9,000 to 9,500 tons per year between 1800 to 1820, yearly output grew to 21,800 tons by the 1830s, and then surged to 60,000 tons by 1850.[31] Much of the explosive growth in world copper production was in the United States, and it centered on copper mines of the Lake Superior district, starting with Hussey's. Whereas in the earlier period Britain produced two-thirds to three-quarters of world production from its Cornwall and Swansea mines, followed by Chile, which picked up production fast in the 1820s, by the 1860s, the new Lake Superior mines of Michigan alone were producing fourteen million pounds of copper per year, 50% of domestic production.[32]

At the time of the Michigan copper discoveries, American mining was limited primarily to Connecticut, Vermont, and Maryland, but in so little quantity that between 1840 and 1845 the United States imported an average of 3,325 tons of unmanufactured copper from the United Kingdom, Chile, and Peru. There were high tariffs on manufactured goods and no tariffs on unmanufactured copper, so most of this came in the form of pigs, sheets and bars.[33] American manufacturers in the East were satisfied with this formula, but the lack of tariffs on raw copper did little to encourage American mining.

The year 1845 was the critical year when Michigan's Lake Superior copper began to hit the market and changed the equation. In addition to driving the growth in copper production and capturing a large share of the domestic market, between 1855 and 1861 30-80% of Michigan copper was shipped for foreign consumption, where its high quality was prized for military and artistic purposes.[34] The United States switched from being a net importer to an exporter. Further support for domestic copper production came in 1861 with the imposition of a 2% tariff on imported copper pigs, bars, and sheets. Combined with the disruption of the Civil War, copper imports fell by 90% in 1862.[35]

The following table shows the exponential growth of the Michigan copper output in the first twenty years, from virtually nil to over thirteen million pounds per year in 1866:

TABLE 8
MICHIGAN OUTPUT OF COPPER AND VALUE OF OUTPUT, 1845–1946

Year	Mine Output[a] (Thousands of Pounds)	Smelter Output[b] (Thousands of Pounds)	Average Price[c] (Cents per Pound)	Estimated Value[d] (Thousands of Dollars)
1845		27	18.5	5
1846		58	17.2	10
1847	Total	477	11.5	50
1848	previous	1,033	19.5	200
1849	to	1,505	22.3	340
1850	1855:	1,281	22.0	280
1851	13,419	1,745	16.6	290
1852		1,744	22.0	380
1853		2,905	22.0	640
1854		4,075	22.0	900
1855	5,820	5,808	27.0	1,570
1856	7,752	8,212	27.0	2,220
1857	9,708	9,531	25.0	2,380
1858	9,023	9,157	23.0	2,110
1859	9,000	8,926	22.0	1,960
1860	11,792	12,069	22.3[e]	2,690
1861	14,842	15,037	19.1	2,870
1862	13,648	13,586	25.8	3,510
1863	12,812	12,985	32.9	4,270
1864	12,403	12,490	46.3	5,780
1865	14,047	14,358	36.3	5,210
1866	13,240	13,749	31.8	4,370
Subtotal 1845–1866	147,506	150,758	27.9	42,035

Growth in Michigan copper production 1845-1866[36]

But in 1843, when Curtis Hussey sent John Hays to Copper Harbor the sea change of 1845 was distant. With the political issues settled, a federal structure in place for claims, a growing demand for copper, and evidence of substantial copper deposits in Michigan, the mining claims rush was on, ultimately driving the vast growth in copper production that began in 1845. In the summer of 1843, in a bar in Copper Harbor, the newly arrived Hays ran into a Bostonian named Jim Raymond who had filed for three claims on the Keweenaw Peninsula. Hays cut a deal for one-sixth of all three claims for $1,000, but when Hays returned to Pittsburgh with the deal, Hussey decided to go bigger.[37] Instead of settling for one-sixth, he persuaded three other Pittsburgh investors to join him: Dr. Charles Avery, Thomas M. Howe, and Dr. William Petitt.

Together these four men controlled two-thirds of the new partnership. Raymond's remaining original backers, Charles Scudder and Thomas Jones of Boston controlled the other one-third, as Raymond shortly backed out and opened a saloon and hotel. Hays was to get one-fourth of the profits from mining and smelting as his share.[38] The financial structure changed throughout the critical first five years: Originally an 1843 partnership, operating from May 13, 1844 as the Pittsburgh & Boston Mining Company, then a joint-stock company on May 20, 1845, the company finally became a Michigan corporation on March 18, 1848 capitalized at $150,000, six thousand shares at $25 per share.[39] The shareholders at this incorporation were Avery, Hussey, Howe, and Thomas Bakewell from Pittsburgh, Charles Scudder from Boston, and George C. Bates from Detroit.[40]

If transportation to the copper country was difficult during the summer, with the only practical access by water and requiring bypassing the rapids below Sault St. Marie, conditions were next to impossible during the winter. Harbors and rivers froze and the land access through the Michigan and Wisconsin wilderness to Detroit was even less hospitable. Returning in the spring of 1844 with a crew, Hays decided to work the claim at Copper Harbor, which showed promise.[41] Hussey himself made the journey to Copper Harbor in 1844 to inspect the new venture.[42]

Two shafts were sunk, and promising deposits were mined, but the vein ran out at 120 feet and the mine was abandoned. Having spent $28,000 in the 1844 and 1845 seasons, the only return was $2,968.[43] This type of strike was common in the area, the result of finding near the surface "deceitful overflow deposits"[44] of mass copper or "float copper" that had been deposited by glaciers[45] rather than the real lode. Despite the failure of the Copper Harbor mine, Hussey later proudly wrote of himself and the company he led, the Pittsburgh and Boston Mining Company:

> The first regular mining shaft ever attempted in the country was sunk in 1844 under the direction of the present President of this company.[46]

Hays then got permission to try the second of the three claims, twenty-five miles down the peninsula from Copper Harbor. Copper was discovered on a 200- foot cliff above a branch of the Eagle River. In retrospect, several people claimed to have discovered the deposits there, but it is likely that Hays deserves primary credit.[47] Led by a party under a "Mr. Cheny" the explorers traced the vein from several inches at the top of the cliff to two feet wide halfway down. United States surveyors Charles T. Jackson and J.D. Whitney visited and advised digging at the base. The miners dug horizontally into the cliff and at 70 feet and struck a mass of pure copper, the first mass of native copper ever discovered in the Lake Superior region.[48]

The miners found it easy at first to burn off the extracted rock to free the mass copper to which it adhered. When the horizontal shaft ran past the vein, they had to drill vertically, break up the masses of copper and hoist using the system of Edwin J. Hurlburt, later of the even more successful Calumet mine.[49] In 1846, the Cliff Mine opened, but the company spent $66,128 on all their Copper Country mining operations and took in only $8,870 in sales for that year.[50] At this point the investors had put up $110,000 since 1844 specifically for the Cliff in the form of an assessment on the $150,000 capital represented by the 6000 shares held by the stockholders. With no profit in sight, the Boston investors wavered at sinking more money into the venture, but the Pittsburgh contingent was cautiously game to go on. Turning to Captain Edward Jennings, the Cliff superintendent, who was of Cornish mining heritage, Charles Avery asked how deep Cornish mines went. The Cliff was at 700 feet. Jennings replied that 700 feet was not deep enough, that copper was seldom found above 800 feet. Avery checked with his banker and was in for an additional $60,000.[51] The gamble paid off. In the1847 season, Cliff extracted 1,500,000 pounds of copper. In May of 1848 alone, the Cliff supplied 400,000 pounds.[52] The mine began clearing $20,000 net profit every month.[53] In 1849, the Pittsburgh and Boston Mining Company paid a dividend of $10 per share on its 6000 shares, a profit to the investors of $60,000 and the first ever dividend for a North American copper mine.[54]

The differing perspectives of the Boston and Pittsburgh interests foreshadow Eastern vs. Western views of industry that were to surface regularly throughout Hussey's careers in copper and steel, with Hussey continually championing the "Western" view. In the case of sinking even more capital into the Cliff Mine in 1846, it was simply a difference of willingness of the Westerners to accept more risk than the Bostonians, but the Westerners tended to differ with the easterners on numerous fronts: tariffs, technological innovation, and marketing among them, with the westerners typically adhering to what became the more modern, late 19th- century view of how best to advance industrial growth.

With the Cliff Mine at the forefront, Michigan quickly became the center of American copper mining. The following table compares Michigan output to total U.S. and world production for the years 1846-1866 when the Cliff Mine was most productive:

TABLE 6
WORLD, UNITED STATES, AND MICHIGAN OUTPUT OF NEW COPPER, 1845–1946
(Thousands of Pounds)

Year	World [a]	United States [b]	Michigan [c]	Percentage Michigan of U.S.
1845	98,762	224 [d]	27 [e]	12.1
1846	"	336	58	17.3
1847	"	672	477	71.0
1848	"	1,120	1,033	92.2
1849	"	1,568	1,505	96.0
1850	"	1,456	1,281	88.0
1851	151,816	2,016	1,745	86.6
1852	"	2,464	1,744	70.8
1853	"	4,480	2,905	64.8
1854	"	5,040	4,075	80.9
1855	"	6,720	5,808	86.4
1856	"	8,960	8,212	91.7
1857	"	10,752	9,531	88.6
1858	"	12,320	9,157	74.3
1859	"	14,112	8,926	63.3
1860	"	16,128	12,069	74.8
1861	229,868	16,800	15,037	89.5
1862	"	21,160	13,586	64.2
1863	"	19,040	12,985	68.2
1864	"	17,920	12,490	69.7
1865	"	19,040	14,358	75.4
1866	"	19,936	13,749	69.0
Subtotal 1845–1866	3,480,040	202,264	150,758	74.5

World, United States, and Michigan copper output, 1845-1866, the effective life of the Cliff Mine[55]

From virtually no world share of copper production in 1845, by 1866 the United States was producing nearly 10% of a vastly larger world output and Michigan was supplying 69% of U.S. copper.

The Cliff Mine prospered from this growth. From 1849 through 1870, just before its sale, the Cliff provided profits of $2,327,660[56] on the original investment of $110,000. That the early years were the best is reflected in an 1857 account that cites the 1855 Directors' report announcing that through 1855, profits from copper sales from the mine had been $1,405,719 on sales of $2,120,101.

Dividends through 1855 had totaled $720,000, with $180,000 more expected in 1856. That year the Cliff Mine employed 445 men, about half of whom were miners earning an average of $37.37 per month.[57]

The following table shows the profits from the Cliff Mine from 1849 through 1866, after which it had only one profitable year before being sold in December 1871 for $100,000[58]:

TABLE 12 (Continued)
DIVIDEND PAYMENTS — ALL MICHIGAN COPPER MINING COMPANIES. (B) 1849-1866
(In Thousands of Dollars)

Year	Cliff	Minesota	National	Pewabic	Quincy	Franklin	Central	Copper Falls	Total
1849	60	....	....	....	....	....	....	..	60
1850	84	....	....	...	....	....	....	..	84
1851	60	....	....	....	....	....	....	..	60
1852	60	....	....	....	....	....	....	..	60
1853	90	....	....	....	....	....	....	..	90
1854	108	90	....	....	....	....	....	..	198
1855	78	90	....	....	....	....	....	..	168
1856	180	200	....	....	....	....	....	..	380
1857	180	300	....	....	....	....	....	..	480
1858	160	300	....	....	....	....	....	..	460
1859	180	180	....	....	....	....	....	..	360
1860	...	120	....	....	....	....	....	..	120
1861	80	100	80	....	....	....	....	..	260
1862	80	160	80	60	60	....	....	..	440
1863	180	160	....	120	200	60	....	..	720
1864	320	60	80	200	280	100	50	60	1,150
1865	200	....	40	....	160	60	50	..	510
1866	120	....	....	....	....	....	50	..	170
Total	2,220	1,760	280	380	700	220	150	60	5,770

[912]

Dividend payments for the Cliff and other Michigan copper mines 1849-1866[59]

The wildly successful mine not only generated enormous cash profits but also drove the stock of the Pittsburgh and Boston Mining Corporation to astronomical levels. An account of the mine's success as of 1855 notes that the actual cash investment was only $110,000 and that the stock had appreciated considerably by the time of this report in 1857:

> The stock of this Company is $150,000, divided into 6000 shares of $25 each; of which $110,000 only has been called in, or what is equal to $18.50 per share: and yet, such has been the success attending the operations of the company, that we notice the market value of the shares quoted in Boston at $250.[60]

In 1849 the Mining Engineers Foster and Whitney produced a series of drawings and sketches that showed the burgeoning activity around the Cliff Mine Their sketch of the Cliff Mine shows the variety of above-ground activity associated with the venture:

Sketch of the Cliff Mine surface 1849[61]

The Foster & Whitney map shows the many buildings on the site:

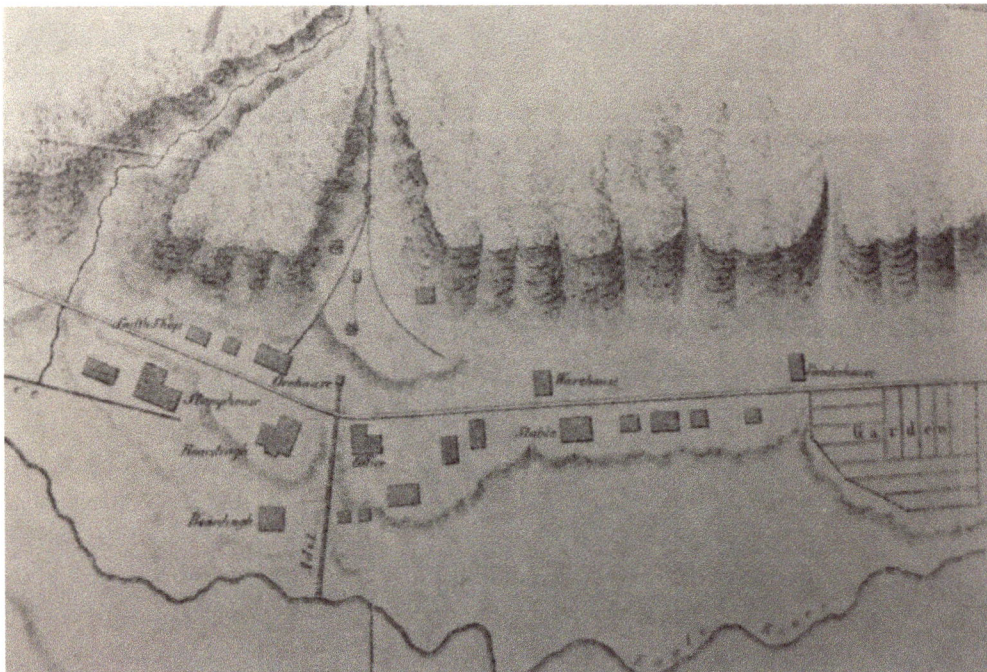

Map of the Cliff Mine buildings in 1849[6]

The following drawing by Foster and Whitney shows a cross-section of the mine in its early years:

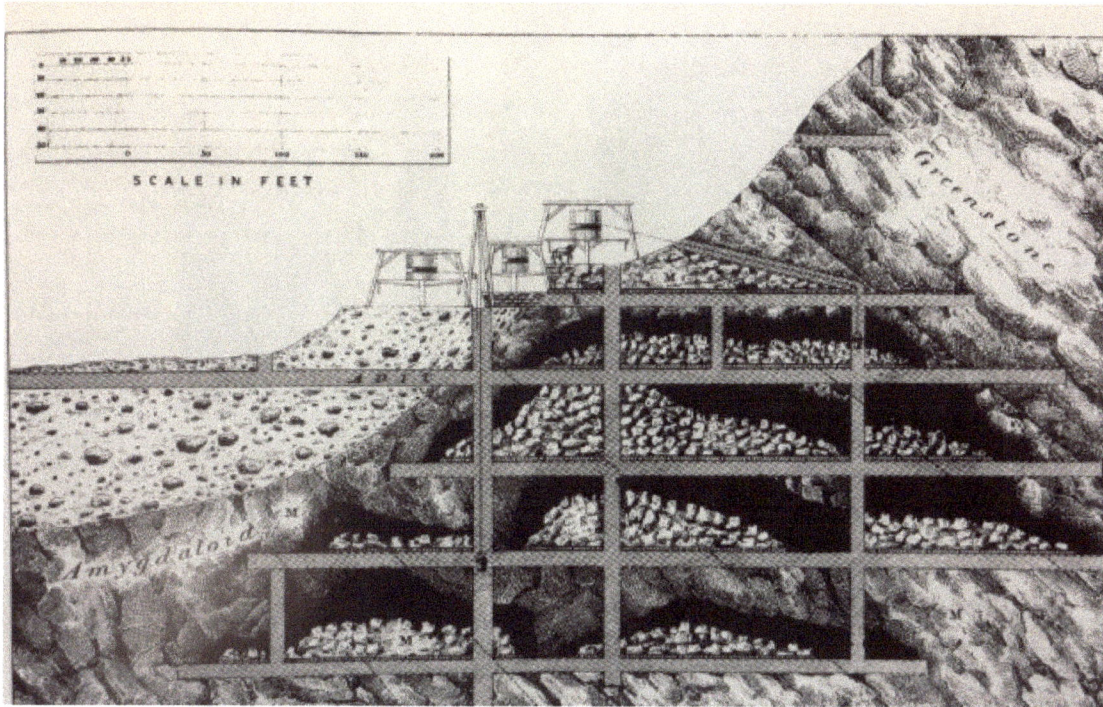

Cliff Mine shafts in 1849[63]

Throughout his career, Hussey ardently publicized his industrial activities and the goods they produced. While there is no evidence that he was directly responsible for the publicity that came from the Foster and Whitney prints, their publication coincided with his strong belief in marketing. Not coincidentally, the most famous publicist of the time, *New York Tribune* celebrity publisher Horace Greeley, was intrigued by the Michigan mines and even visited the Keweenaw Peninsula in 1847, where he visited ten mines, including the Cliff and gave glowing reviews of the operations, characterizing the Cliff as having "no rival in this region nor in the world".[64] Greeley was, of course, the man who coined the motto "Go West, young man."

As the first American copper operation that was a true mine, the Cliff Mine required many advances in technology and management. Necessary technical advances included installing the first steam-winding machine in 1850 to hoist the ore mechanically rather than by horse. By 1858 skips holding up to 2.5 tons of rocks replaced kibbles that could hold only up to a ton. [65]

In the early drawing of the Cliff Mine above, the deepest shaft was less than 300 feet. By the 1860s, when the mine reached 1500 feet[66], the 1000-foot ladders which the miners clambered up and down were no longer practical and the Cliff installed the first American mining "man engine" (elevator), shown below.

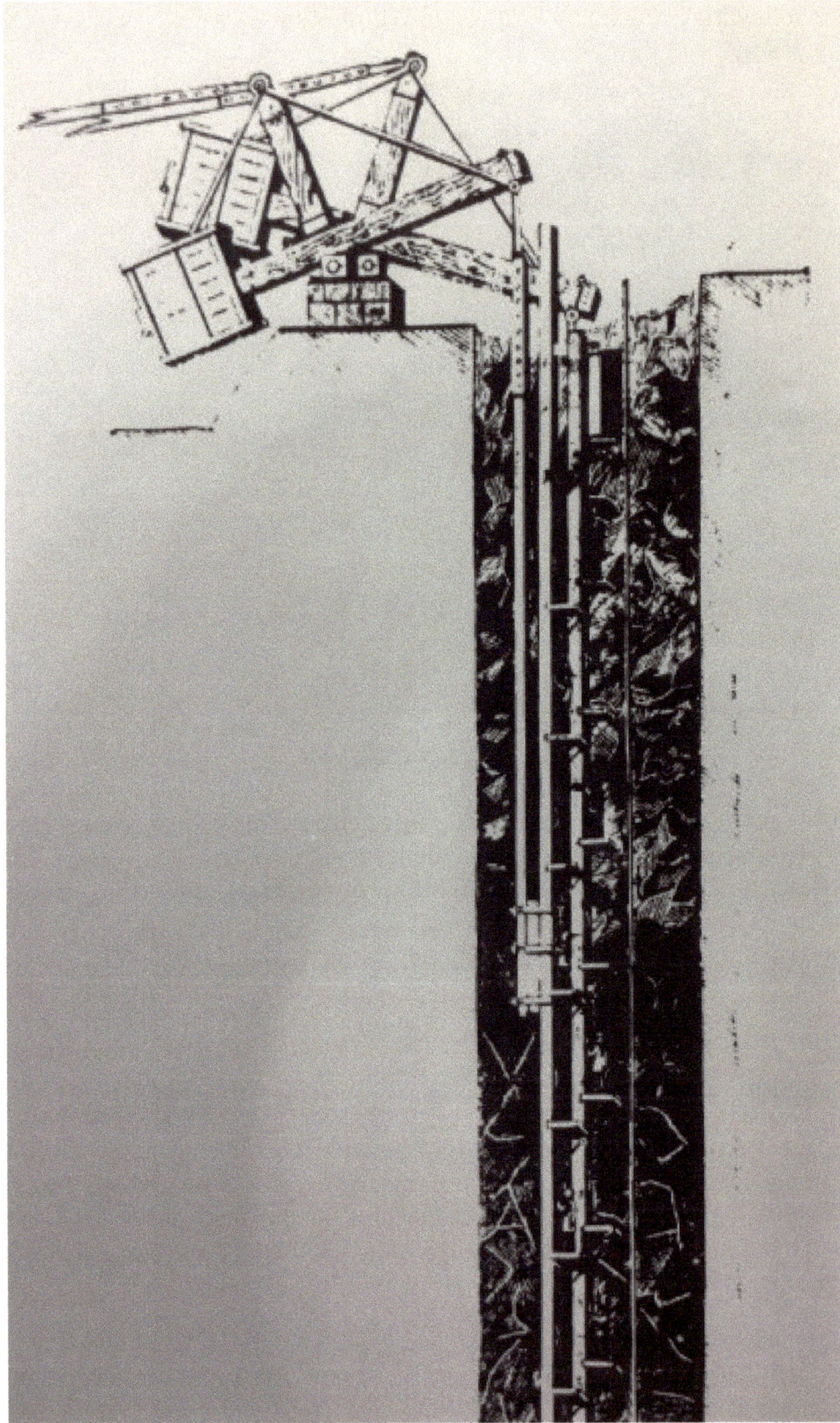

Drawing of the first "man engine" elevator, installed at the Cliff Mine in 1865[67]

Management innovations for the massive enterprise included a sophisticated organization into department heads for each mining activity, for example, having a management structure that was divided into departments.[68]

Two other critical factors that forced Hussey and the Cliff to innovate were the distance of Michigan lands from the traditional Eastern smelting factories and the size and composition of the chunks of mined copper. Because the journey was long and costly, the prevailing arrangement was for mine owners to extend long- term credit of up to four months to the buyers of the copper in the East[69]. But by 1853, the Cliff had already disrupted this pattern and was demanding and getting cash and carry,[70] a considerable cash-flow advantage. Presumably, one reason that the Cliff could make this demand was that Hussey was now smelting the copper and producing copper products himself at his Pittsburgh Copper and Brass Rolling mills and at another smelting facility in Cleveland run by his brother Joseph Hussey, which operated from 1850 to 1867.[71]

The new smelters and a unique furnace that Hussey invented to handle the copper ore, in turn, were an answer to yet another problem encountered by the copper from the Cliff: its composition. The implications of shipping distance and the nature of the copper become clearer as the story of the Pittsburgh Copper and Brass Works unfolds in the next section.

Meanwhile, another transportation issue had to be resolved. The remote and difficult route encountered by Hays and Hussey on their separate trips to Copper Harbor was even more daunting for shipping the copper and other ore from Lake Superior to Detroit, Cleveland, Pittsburgh or the East. As early as 1839, the state of Michigan had authorized and begun digging a canal to bypass the rapids below Sault St. Marie. The federal government put a halt to this effort,[72] but efforts continued in the following decade to convince Congress to authorize Michigan to build the canal. Hussey and other Pittsburgh industrialists were instrumental in the petition process. In January 1852 at a meeting chaired by Mayor John B. Guthrie of Pittsburgh organized the Pittsburgh effort.

The Hussey interests were well represented. In addition to Hussey himself, James M. Cooper, who later partnered in Hussey's steel business, served as secretary of the committee and Charles Avery attended and spoke. Hussey introduced a series of resolutions to support the petition to Congress for a canal to bypass the rapids. The resolutions explicitly cited the need to support the growing copper and iron mining operations on Lake Superior. The resolutions concluded that the canal "would open up navigation from the head of Lake Superior to the St. Lawrence and Atlantic and by the Illinois Canal and the Mississippi to the Gulf of Mexico." A committee of fourteen, including Hussey, was appointed to prepare a memorial to Congress and to gather signatures for it.[73] Hussey is never directly quoted, nor does the article explain who drafted the resolutions that he introduced.

This pattern characterized Hussey's entire public life. In his businesses, his founding role is clear. But particularly with respect to his civic involvement later in life, he was often present at the inception of some initiative or campaign, usually as a formal leader and substantial financial supporter, but seldom as the acknowledged original force behind the venture or commentator on it.

Congress finally agreed, passing an act on August 21, 1852, which granted Michigan 750,000 acres to support the building of the canal and setting standards for the canal dimensions.[74] The first iteration of the Soo Locks was completed in May 1855; it was operated by the State of Michigan until transferred to the U.S. Army in 1881. Today the locks are part of a 1.6-mile canal formally named the St. Mary's Falls Canal. The entire canal, including the locks, is owned and maintained by the United States Army Corps of Engineers, which provides free passage.[75] The Keweenaw Peninsula remained isolated and distant, but the intolerable bottleneck of the St. Mary River rapids was removed.

Hussey and his partners were extraordinarily lucky in the strike at the Cliff Mine. Mining is highly speculative and requires enormous capital expenses and considerable time before it becomes clear whether or not the effort pays. Of the 94 copper mines in the area during the years 1844-1866, only eight ever paid a dividend and only six paid more in dividends above the assessments required of the stockholders to develop: Cliff, Minesota[1], Quincy, Prewabic, National, and Franklin.[76] The Pittsburgh investors invested in many more mines. Hussey, Howe, or Avery were officers in the North Western Mining Company, Mass Mining Company, Great Western Mining Company, Great Western Mining Company, Miscowaubik Mining Company, Aztec Mining Co, Copper Harbor Mining Co, Mann Mining Co, Swampscott Mining Co, National Mining Co, Adventure Mining Co, and Central Mining Co. Hussey also went to California in 1849 to investigate mining possibilities and also invested in gold, copper and silver mines in Georgia, Colorado, Utah, New Mexico, Arizona, Nevada, British Columbia, Mexico, and elsewhere, though never with any success approaching his Cliff Mine strike.[77] See the Appendix ("Hussey's Other Enterprises") for a partial list of Hussey's mining ventures and other businesses.

Despite the apparent dangers of the wildly speculative mining business, Gates notes that "...the Cliff management was sometimes criticized as being too conservative. In any case, Dr. Hussey and his associates were much more circumspect in their operations."[78] This seems a strange characterization for such a pioneering and uncharted venture, not to mention the fact that Hussey invested in dozens of other mines, mostly unsuccessfully. More likely, it attests to the fact that Hussey and his partners in the Cliff Mine acted prudently and methodically in those areas in which they had some real possibility of exercising control. They were not freebooters.

The Michigan mines in the 1840s and 1850s were the heart of the exponential growth of copper production to meet the new worldwide demand, and the Cliff Mine was where it all started. Getting the copper out of the ground was only the first part of the story; next, Hussey turned from mining to copper production, revolutionizing the smelting process to turn the mined copper into metal to create products.

---

[1] "Minesota" is not a misspelling, although it clearly was when the mine was so named.

Pittsburgh Copper & Brass Rolling Mill and C.G. Hussey & Co.

In 1849, Hussey founded the Pittsburgh Copper & Brass Rolling Mill under the ownership of a new company, C.G. Hussey & Co. Hussey contributed $30,000, which was matched by Avery, who lent the money at ten percent interest to Howe, who thereby owned half.[79] Distance from the traditional smelters was one reason for opening the rolling mill nearer the source, but problems related to the nature of the copper discovered at the Cliff Mine was another direct cause. Copper is trapped in the ground in a variety of configurations. In the Michigan copper area, three types of copper deposits were found:

- Amygdaloid, which is igneous rock with pure metal in amygdules, almond shaped cavities into which the molten copper had flowed and hardened. This was the type found at the Prebawic Mine.

- Conglomerate, which is puddingstone pebbles cemented together with pure copper metal. This was found at Calumet, the greatest of all Michigan copper mines, discovered in the late 1860s.

- Mass is the least complicated of the three types. It is a solid piece of native or pure copper weighing 100 pounds or more and embedded in a rock matrix. This was the type found at Cliff and Minesota and was unheard of before in America.[80]

The first discoveries in the Michigan lands were of mass copper deposits near the surface, not the amygdaloid or conglomerate that later came to be the mainstay of American copper mining. However, these first mass copper deposits turned out to be freaks, minor spillover from the original formation of copper masses or glacial deposits. All three Lake Superior copper configurations ran to great depth and were not typically at surface, and they were quite different than how copper was found elsewhere in the world where sulfur or other undesirable elements complicated the smelting.[81]

While these unheard-of mass copper deposits of pure copper presented enormous opportunities, the mining process was complicated. The masses were often so big that they not only had to be freed from surrounding rock, but also had to be chiseled into smaller pieces to be removed, put into kibbles (buckets) and pulled to the surface, at first by horses, but by the early 1850s, by steam engines. For pieces of mass copper that were still adhered to rock, the stamping process took over: large iron stampers crushed the copper and any adhering rock into smaller pieces, from which chunks of copper were separated by a flow of water.[82]

Once the ore was out of the ground and stamped into small enough pieces to be shipped, it needed to be smelted to separate the copper from rock and any other elements. There were three early attempts at smelting in the Keweenaw Peninsula area in 1846-49: Professor James T. Hodges on the Gratiot River, the Suffolk Mining Company southeast of the Eagle River, and the Ohio and Isle Royale Mining Company; all failed.[83] So, what little was mined at Lake Superior had to be shipped east to be smelted. Most went to Paul Revere's Point Shirley mill at Winthrop, Massachusetts, near Boston, or to Levi Hollingsworth's Baltimore works.[84] The initial Cliff Mine output went to Point Shirley.[85]

In addition to mining problems related to the sheer size of the pure mass copper deposits, other issues arose. Transportation costs to the east were very high, $18 to $20 per ton.[86] This compared to copper coming from Chile at $15 per ton and Cuba at $6 per ton.[87] Of more serious concern, neither the Baltimore nor the Point Shirley smelters could handle the large chunks of pure copper coming from Michigan.

Previously, all smelting had been of copper ore fed in through small side doors in the furnaces. At Baltimore in 1847, in order to accommodate the large blocks of pure copper from the Cliff, even when cut for shipping into chunks one ton or less from masses that can run to 100 tons, the owners built a larger furnace with doors on either side, then dragged the new larger copper masses through, bricking up the entry door and firing. This constantly damaged the furnaces, requiring extensive rebuilding.

Similar failures occurred at the Fort Pitt Foundry in 1848, where they tried the existing ordinary side-door refining cannon furnace, but removed the arched roof, placed the mass inside, then rebuilt the arch. The result was yet another problem: too much slag because of the slow heating and melting of the mass.[88]

The process of smelting mass copper, such as that found at the Cliff, was not as simple as it seemed. The blocks were so large that they were difficult to melt. Even worse, the process produced much copper oxide slag (the impurities that separate out during smelting) that defeated the supposed benefit of starting with pure copper. Additional refining steps would be necessary and did not seem economically practical.[89] Revere, no more experienced than Baltimore in smelting mass copper, wanted to charge Hussey $80 per ton.[90] Finally, undeterred by these seemingly intractable problems, Hussey decided to build his own smelting works, founding C.G. Hussey & Co in 1848 to build a local smelter and rolling mill on the Monongahela a mile north of Pittsburgh, operating as the Pittsburgh and Boston Copper & Brass Rolling Works.[91]

The rolling mill, shown on the 1882 map below, remained off Second Avenue from 1848 for more than a century, flanked by other iron and copper works along the Monongahela River. It passed out of the Hussey family in 1936, and the business was moved to Leetsdale PA in 1964, where it remains today, as Hussey Copper,[92] nearly a century and three quarters after its founding. The Pittsburgh Technology Center now occupies the old site along the Monongahela River.

1882 map showing C. G. Hussey & Co.'s Pittsburgh Copper & Brass Rolling Mills[93]

Other western consumers of Cliff copper were smelters in Detroit and the Cleveland smelter run by his brother. By shipping the ore across Lake Erie to Cleveland, and then to Hussey's Pittsburgh works, transportation costs were cut in half.[94] By 1881, most of the local smelting facilities that followed Hussey's were gone. Only three smelters remained processing the kind of pure and highly prized native copper found at the Cliff, Hussey's Pittsburgh rolling mill and two belonging to the Detroit and Lake Superior Copper Company,[95] All, including the others that came and went after the founding of Pittsburgh Copper and Brass Rolling Mills, were modeled after Hussey's.[96] By the 1880s the Cliff Mine was sold and out of business and Hussey's rolling mill was consuming copper from sources other than the Cliff.

Hussey not only started a copper smelter, but he revolutionized the smelting process that was both better suited to large masses of copper and less expensive to smelt. To overcome the dual problems of damage to the furnaces because of size and of excessive slag that resulted from slow melting of such large copper masses, he hit upon the strategy of using two existing European technologies: moveable lids and reverberatory furnaces,[97] two innovations that defined copper smelting for the next 100 years in the United States.[98]

Hussey had heard about furnaces with moveable lids, supported by cranes, used in large German furnaces for the cupellation of silver lead. Lowering the mass copper after removing the lid would solve the problem of getting it into the furnace without dragging it in and damaging the furnace.[99] A reverberatory furnace is one in which the flame is reflected off the roof of the furnace onto the material being treated. This separates the material being worked on (the copper) from the source of the heat, which better controls the process. Any resulting slag, or molten rock, is skimmed off. Other impurities are eliminated by splashing the copper into the air to be burned out by oxidation. Oxygen, which would combine with the copper to produce undesirable copper oxide ("black copper"), is eliminated by introducing hardwood to the molten mass. The carbon in the wood unites with the oxygen. The result is that mineral containing 65 to 75 per cent copper produces copper of 99 per cent purity.[100]

Accounts differ as to who was responsible for Hussey adopting the reverberatory furnace technology.[102] Hussey himself gets credit in most sources, which in fact is true in that it was his typical curiosity and entrepreneurial energy that put it all together and thereby guaranteed his fortune.

The following diagram shows the principles of a reverberatory furnace:

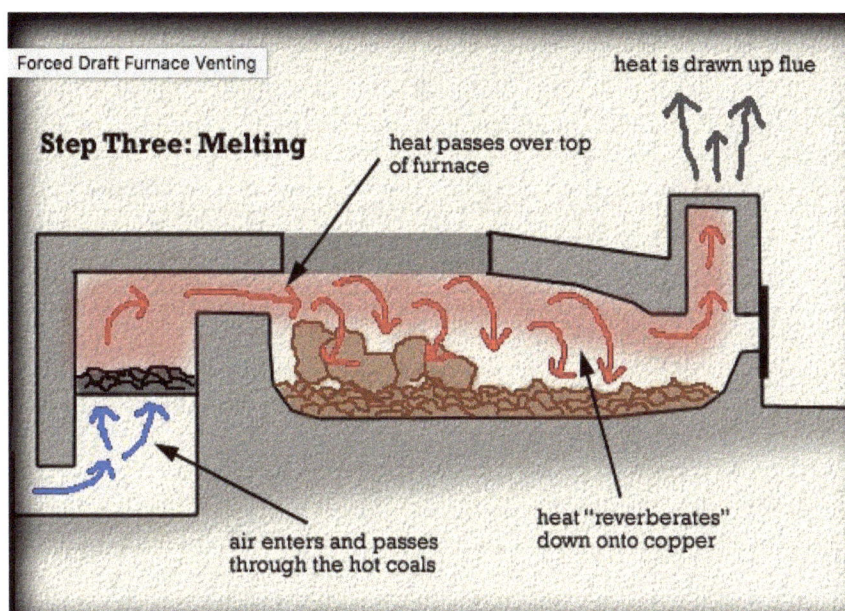

Forced Draft Furnace Venting

Step Three: Melting

heat passes over top of furnace

heat is drawn up flue

heat "reverberates" down onto copper

air enters and passes through the hot coals

Simple diagram of a reverberatory furnace, showing how heat source (the coal) is kept separate from the charge (the copper) to minimize slag (the waste resulting from the smelting).[101]

Presumably, the same technical innovations were included in the copper smelting works build at Cleveland in 1850 by Hussey's brother, Joseph, as J. G. Hussey & Co. This operation was closer to the Cliff Mine but never seems to have fulfilled its promise, closing in 1867.[103] Since Cleveland was better located than Pittsburgh to handle the Michigan output, this failure presumably speaks to the disparity in the managerial capabilities of Joseph and C.G. Hussey.

C.G. Hussey & Co was not only the owner of the Pittsburgh Copper and Brass Rolling Mill but served an additional role as the third layer in Hussey's vertically integrated copper enterprises. With offices at 49 Fifth Avenue and a warehouse at 37 Fifth Avenue, and with warehouses in Philadelphia, New York, and Boston, it served as the marketing and sales vehicle for the output of the rolling mill.

Advertisements for the various products appeared regularly in the Pittsburgh newspapers throughout Hussey's lifetime. Eventually, the rolling works themselves were recognized simply as "C.G. Hussey & Co Works".

The following plate shows the rolling mill in full production and notes also that C.G Hussey & Co. also maintained a warehouse on Fifth Avenue:

Nineteenth century depiction of Hussey's Pittsburgh Copper and Brass Rolling Mills[104]

Hussey's Fifth Avenue headquarters itself was celebrated in a front-page article announcing its 1859 opening in the Pittsburgh Daily post, accompanied by this view of the "Iron Bank Building":

THE IRON BANK BUILDING,

Fifth Street, between Wood and Market, Pittsburgh,

COMMENCED JULY 3d, 1858, AND COMPLETED WITHIN THE YEAR.

PROPRIETORS

Wm. Bagaley, The Allegheny Bank, The Pittsburgh & Boston Mining Co., C. G. Hussey & Co.

ARCHITECT, CHARLES BARTBURGER.

Hussey's new headquarters on Fifth Avenue, 1859[105]

A few months later the following advertisement announced the opening of the C.G Hussey & Co. headquarters in the new Iron Building at 37 Fifth Avenue, a decade after the founding of the rolling mill. Hussey has minimized the "Bank" branding:

29

Notice of Moving to the Iron Building 1859[106]

Small, nearly identical advertisements appeared regularly in the Pittsburgh Post and the Pittsburgh Daily Commercial throughout the following decades, like this one from 1881:

Recurring advertisement that ran for decades for Hussey copper[107]

By 1876, the C.G. Hussey rolling mills operation was characterized as:

> ...now as large as any in the country. The mills consist of three large buildings and numerous smaller ones, covering an area of about four acres. The operative work is divided into four departments, viz. – rolling mill, brass, smelting, and planishing, requiring a force of one hundred men, three large engines, and other improved mechanisms for planishing, cutting, turning, etc.[108]

The Cliff Mine was played out by the late 1860s, but throughout the following decades C.G. Hussey & Co. and the Pittsburgh Copper and Brass Rolling Mill prospered and supplied Hussey with capital for his other industrial, commercial, and philanthropic ventures.

In 1859 Hussy turned his attention to another nascent industry, one that ultimately dwarfed copper: steel.

Steel

Hussey's pioneer copper mining, smelting, and sales organization ensure his niche in American industrial history, but in the following decade he did it all over again, this time in steel. In 1859 he became the first major producer of American crucible steel, the high-quality tool steel that had previously been available only as an import from England. Moreover, he introduced a simpler and cheaper steel- making process that had not been successfully used anywhere in the world. His contemporaries, right up to Andrew Carnegie, considered him a steel pioneer.

Making Steel

Steel is produced from bars of pig iron. Pig iron is the intermediate product of smelting iron ore. Furnaces are loaded with iron ore, coke, and limestone. The limestone is used as a flux to combine with some of the impurities that are separated when heating the ore and blowing hot air over the charge. Carbon from the coke combines with the oxygen in the heated iron ore to burn off as carbon monoxide, leaving some of the carbon in the melted iron. The liquid iron collects at the bottom and flows out to harden as pig iron.[109].

Pig iron is too hard and brittle to be of much use but can be processed into cast iron, wrought iron, or steel. Cast iron and wrought iron are iron alloys whose main difference in composition is the amount of carbon. Pig iron contains 4-5% carbon, compared to less than 1% for wrought iron and between 2-4% for cast iron.[110] By the 19th-century, carbon was being removed from pig iron to create wrought iron by puddling, which is the process of blowing hot air over the fuel coming into direct contact with the iron (the "charge").[111] In the industrial boom of the mid-19th-century when Hussey turned his attention to steel, both wrought iron and cast iron were used for mass uses, such as construction and railroad rails. Cast iron was cheaper and easier to use, but wrought iron was more malleable to work and less brittle.

Steel, by contrast, was not used in quantity for construction or rails in mid 19th-century, because although it had superior properties to wrought or cast iron, it was extremely expensive to make. The process for creation was similar to that of making wrought or cast iron: by heating the iron bars hot enough to separate out impurities, either by burning them off as gases or separating them into slag (waste which was discarded) while simultaneously managing that the result contained a specific range of carbon for strength.

The result, steel, is both stronger than iron and better able to take and maintain a sharp edge. Steel contains between .5 and 1.5 percent carbon.[112] The key to steel is to remove virtually all impurities such as phosphorous, sulfur, and the iron silicate that remained in its main 19th-century competitor, wrought iron, while controlling the carbon content by either removing the excess carbon down to the correct level or through a combination of removing and replacing carbon to that .5 to 1.5 percent level, depending on what the steel is to be used for.

Steel has been made for millennia, probably starting in the Indian subcontinent around 300 years BCE, but also in Central Asia and the Mideast, and eventually Europe.[113] Historically, two main processes were used to create steel: cementation and crucible. Both, in succession, had a role in the growth of European and then American steel production from the small, specialized steel production in Asia and the Mideast to large-scale modern steel production.

For European steel production from the Middle Ages on, the cementation process was used. The best iron ore was needed to create pig iron, which was then forged into bars and packed between layers of charcoal, then slowly heated. Over the course of days, even weeks, the bars were observed and tested. Iron became steel by the diffusion of impurities such as sulfur and the absorption of just the right amount of carbon from the charcoal. Even then, the bars had to be sorted and recombined according to quality.[114] The lengthy process depended on large amounts of fuel and required highly skilled craftsmen. This ancient process is now termed cementation and the result is blister steel, so called because of the characteristic lumps or bumps on the surface of the output of the firing.[115]

The chemical processes for steel production were not known to those involved in creating steel. Steelmakers learned by trial and error. One variable that they did understand was the ore. They saw that the quality of the iron ore affected the quality of the steel. In Europe, Swedish iron ore came to be the most highly prized raw material. Throughout the weeks of the smelting process, the steel craftsmen had to pull out test bars. They could visually assess that it was properly blistered and after cooling and working the test bars they could test other qualities

The percentage of carbon determines its suitability for the purpose desired, even within one piece. For example, a good sword would have a higher carbon level in the middle of the blade for strength and a lower level near the edge to allow for taking and holding a sharp edge. Once the blister steel was of acceptable quality according to the craftsmen, it had to be forged (beaten) to break off slag that clung to the outside, to smash out additional impurities and to make the steel as uniform as possible by diffusing the carbon evenly. The result of working the blister steel is shear steel, which was ready for manufacture into implements such as weapons, cutlery, or tools.[116] The complexity of the steel-making process, and its trial-and- error quality – it often failed, and the result had to be thrown out or reprocessed – made steel an expensive luxury. Steel knives and forks, chisels, swords, not to mention a suit of armor, were not for the masses.

And so it went for centuries. Then, in 1742 an Englishman, Benjamin Huntsman, invented (or, more accurately, rediscovered and improved on) a process for creating higher quality steel than was possible from simply forging the blister steel into shear steel. Thus was born modern crucible steel. Huntsman placed blister steel bars into clay pots in a furnace and fired the furnace with charcoal.[117] While this cost about one-third more than blister steel, the result was worth it: the exceptionally hot environment melted the blister steel into liquid, which made it far more uniform in quality than that produced from the layered iron and fuel in cementation. The additional slag produced by the higher heat could be raked off the molten mass, and the molten steel could be poured into molds.[118]

The result was crucible steel, also called cast steel (because of the ingots created by pouring into the molds) or tool steel, a term later used to distinguish it from Bessemer steel, about which more later. The introduction of the clay pots added another variable, like the ore, which was again dealt with by trial and error. The clay had to be hard enough to withstand the exceptional high heat but add only minimal impurities to the emerging steel. Even the best mixture of clay and other elements produced pots with a limited lifespan before the process had degenerated them.[119]

The crucible steel produced in the Sheffield England area supplied almost all of the growing demand in the United States in the early 19th-century. The United States only produced a few hundred tons of crucible steel by the 1850s, while imports of Sheffield steel peaked at around 22,000 tons per year in 1860.[120] Again at an American industrial forefront, Hussey founded the firm of Hussey, Wells & Co. in 1859 and in 1860 became the first major producer of American crucible steel.

Early steelmaking in the United States

The earliest attempt at American crucible steel was in 1818, by a firm later known as the Alan Wood Steel Company of Valley Forge, PA, but it was soon abandoned. Garrard brothers in Cincinnati in 1832 followed, showing that it was technically possible to create domestic tool steel through the crucible steel method. In the mid-1840s, Adirondack Iron & Steel Co., in conjunction with an Englishman named Pickslay, flirted with making crucible steel, but the results were unsatisfactory and by 1848 Adirondack had gone back to blister steel exclusively.[121].

As with copper, lowering of tariffs on steel in the second quarter of the 19th-century was a factor in strangling early efforts at the manufacture of quality tool steel. Garrard Brothers failed in 1837 and Adirondack Iron and Steel Company in Jersey City in 1848 probably also gave up in part because of the inability to compete on price with imported steel. The Tariff of 1833, which took all tariffs off imported raw materials, effectively shut Garrard down, and the succeeding Tariffs of 1848 and 1857 maintained the low-tariff policy.[122]

In short, the same forces were at work against domestic steel production as against copper until close to the civil war. Eastern manufacturers requiring tool steel were satisfied with using cheap and high-quality British steel. Southern planters were satisfied with imported British steel products that provided income to Britain to buy Southern cotton.

These allied American interests resisted tariffs, which would raise their costs by forcing them to buy internally. Passage of the Morrill Act 1860 was key to the successful birth of the American crucible steel industry, and Hussey was on the spot when that protection was introduced. Whether or not he recognized that the momentum was moving toward protection of domestic production, his pioneering entry into crucible steel corresponded to his earlier recognition with copper that the interests of Western firms involved in the extraction and processing of raw materials differed from those in the East.

By 1850, annual American steel production was about 6078 tons, of which only 44 were crucible (cast) steel.[123] The rest was the cruder blister or shear steel. As the steel scene shifted to Pittsburgh, several firms tried but failed with crucible steel. Briton Simon Broadmeadow was producing blister steel as early as 1830 but failed with crucible steel. G. & J.H. Schoenberger made some cast (crucible) steel in 1840 but gave up within a year or two. McKelvey & Blair in 1852 became the first large-scale producer of cast steel but it was not of the highest quality,[124] and they ceased production within two years. Singer, Nimick & Co and Pittsburgh Steelworks also succeeded in producing cast steel in 1853 and 1855 respectively.[125] But it was when C.G. Hussey bought the abandoned McKelvey & Blair plant and founded Hussey, Wells & Co at 17th and Penn that America began to compete seriously with England in producing crucible steel.

Hussey, Wells & Company

With the founding of Hussey, Wells & Company, the recurring patterns and themes of C.G. Hussey's serial enterprises repeats one last time: good judgment about an emerging market, willingness to be a technological pioneer, ability to make quick decisions and back them up with considerable resources, and a sharp eye for choosing good collaborators.

To be sure, there were some differences between how Hussey's copper and steel interests were organized. He recruited as investors the bankers James M. Cooper and Thomas M. Howe, both of whom were invested in the Cliff Mine, but he also quickly settled on a young active partner who was not just an employee like Hays. Hussey's first industrial venture, the copper company C.G. Hussey & Co., was owned by Hussey himself, but the steel company was Hussey, Wells & Co.

Calvin Wells had come to Pittsburgh at the age of 20 in 1847 to attend the Western University of Pennsylvania[2] and live with his brother, Rev. Samuel Taggart Wells. In 1850 he met John Hays, who recommended him to Hussey, who in turn hired him after a single interview.[126] Hussey first employed Wells in the copper works and then in 1852 set him up in the pork business as Hussey & Wells to manage the pork packing business still being run out of Gosport, Indiana.[127] When Hussey decided to go into steel in 1859, the company became Hussey, Wells & Co., with Wells as manager.[128] While in partnership with Hussey for the next quarter century, Wells also continued to expand his own entrepreneurial efforts, either alone or with other partners, including firms that manufactured car springs, a natural fit, since they required high quality crucible steel, zinc sheeting, and as president of the Pittsburg Forge & Iron Company. He withdrew from the partnership with Hussey in 1876 and the following year he and others purchased the Philadelphia Press in 1877, later securing a controlling interest.[129] After he left Hussey, Wells & Co that firm was renamed Hussey, Howe, & Co., for one of the original investors, Hussey's old friend Thomas Howe.

---

[2] Later the University of Pittsburgh. Hussey was a trustee from 1864 until his death.

In that quarter century, the partnership with Wells flourished. Hussey's characteristic ability to choose his associates well, make quick but bold decisions, and exercise his uncanny knack for being on the technological edge came together again. Wells had been known since his youth "of a mechanical turn of mind and very handy with tools."[130] Immediately upon planning to go into steel production, Hussey sent Wells east to New Jersey to learn the about crucibles, just as he had sent Hays to Michigan to scout for copper. In particular, he likely sent him to see Joseph Dixon. Dixon, in his home town of Marblehead, Massachusetts, had discovered that graphite (also called plumbago) was ideal for adding to the clay mixture needed to make crucibles that withstood heat without polluting the melting process. Dixon's own efforts to make crucible steel failed,[131] but he relocated to New Jersey and was successfully selling his crucibles for copper and brass which would have brought Dixon to Hussey's attention:

> It was probably Dr. Hussey... who first thought that the new Dixon crucibles made of graphite mixed with Klingenberg clay from Germany might change crucible steel picture in Pittsburgh. At least we know that Dr. Hussey acted first.[132]

Having studied the crucible steel-manufacturing process, and adopting the plumbago solution for the crucibles, Wells returned to Pittsburgh and supervised the reconstruction of the old McKelvey and Blair steelworks at 17th and Penn. The massive plant soon covered several acres of land in downtown Pittsburgh just south of the Allegheny River, as depicted in this elegant 1870 lithograph:

Lithograph of Hussey, Wells & Co. Steelworks at 17th & Penn, c. 1870[133]

The plant occupied land conveniently close to both a rail line and the Allegheny River in downtown Pittsburgh:

Map of Hussey, Wells & Co. at 17th & Penn, 1872[134]

In addition to adopting the best crucible technology, Hussey's other technological breakthrough was his adoption of the so-called "direct method" of producing crucible steel. From the time of Huntsman, crucible steel required a two- step "conversion" process to turn the pig iron bars into steel (pig iron being the crudely refined, brittle, first processing of iron ore): first, the iron had to be converted into blister steel through the old cementation process, then, the blister steel was transformed in crucibles into cast steel.

Cutting out the interim step of producing blister steel would save time and money.

An Englishman held a patent on a direct method as early as 1839 and another Englishman, Pickslay, had attempted the process for Adirondack Iron & Steel in 1848, but had failed.[135] From the beginning, Hussey used the direct method. The direct process depended on the improved crucibles for its success. The Dixon- inspired crucibles provided multiple advantages. They transmitted heat better, which saved fuel. There was also less contamination of the molten steel from the crucibles. Finally, they were more durable, which not only saved on the cost of the crucibles but had the unexpected advantage of producing better steel: steel produced in new crucibles turned out to be of lower quality than if produced in later uses of the same crucible.[136]

Contemporary accounts indicate strong resistance to Hussey's introduction of the direct method, though without explanation as to the objections:

> This 'direct process' was attacked bitterly by the agents of English steel in New York and elsewhere.[137]

While his English competitors may have thought his technology foolish, more likely, it was less the direct process which troubled the English steelmakers and the American businesses which depended on imported English tool steel, but rather that there was a nascent crucible steel business at all that was beginning to compete with them. Hussey seems to have been unconcerned, relying on his judgment in new technologies and his own resources, financial and in terms of personnel. In any case, other steelmakers quickly followed upon his success, and all eventually adopted this process for producing cast steel in crucibles directly from pig iron, or from cheaper grades of steel.

With the energetic Wells managing the steelworks using the latest technology, Hussey, Wells & Co. began the first serious crucible steel manufacturing in the United States. Hussey is said to have spent $400,000 initially, spending up to $2 million by 1870 on his steelworks.[138] Others followed, but Hussey, Wells & Co. and its successors Hussey, Howe & Co. (1876) and Howe, Brown & Co. (1888), the latter formed when Hussey retired from steel, remained key players until the consolidation of the crucible steel industry at the turn of the 20th century. As Gilmer summed up the arc of crucible steel manufacturing in the second half of the 19th- century:

> ...the first firm to engage successfully in the manufacture of crucible steel became part of the Crucible Steel Company of America on its founding in 1900. This firm was Hussey, Wells & Co, of Pittsburgh, later know as Howe, Brown, & Co.[139]

Or, as Casson put it:

> There was little or no steel made in Pittsburgh or in any other American city until 1861, when the Morrill tariff shut out the English steel and gave our steelmakers a start. The firm of Hussey, Wells & Co., of Pittsburgh, was the first to break down the prejudice that existed against American steel. Close on their heels came such men as Schoenberger, Spang, Chalfant, Singer, Nimick, Gregory, and Park.[40]

Finally, Swank:

> The manufacture in this country of crucible cast steel of the best grades may be said to be established on a firm basis after Hussey, Wells & Co., Park Brothers & Co., and Gregory & Co. in the years 1860, 1862, and 1863, respectively succeeded in making it of uniform quality as a regular product.[141]

Despite the technological success of Hussey's direct process, it was not easy to erase the image of American crucible steel as being inferior to imported steel, most notably the English steel typically referred to as Sheffield steel. Tweedale quotes Hussey as "begging" for a chance to prove the quality of his steel.[142] Beyond simply begging, Hussey characteristically took the initiative, actively soliciting testimonials from those using the steel of Hussey, Wells & Company. In 1866 the company published a twenty-eight-page booklet filled with one or two paragraph customer recommendations. The solicited testimonies are dated from 1864 to 1866, and all emphasize that Hussey's steel is equal or better to the best steel of the day. Many of them specifically compare the quality to imported steel, as in this succinct 1864 letter from the Indiana firm of Bement & Webster:

> Gentlemen – We have used your Steel about two years and a half, and find it to be the best we ever worked. It is clear from seams. We consider it better than English Steel.[143]

Note that the letter-writer states that he has been using Hussey steel for more than two years, which means from at least 1862, barely two years after Hussey, Wells & Co. began production. Hussey was soliciting testimony from the beginning and using modern marketing techniques in the same way he had with copper.

Other evidence of the pioneering success of steel produced by Hussey, Wells & Co. include an 1864 *Scientific American* article, which quotes the *Boston Commercial Bulletin* describing a visit to the steelworks. In addition to repeating the assertion that Hussey's steel was the first American product to be competitive with, in fact superior to, British steel, the *Boston Commercial Bulletin* correspondent supplies detail about the plant capacity:

> From twelve small furnaces in 1859, with about twenty-five men, the Hussey, Wells & Co.'s works have increased to ninety furnaces now in full operation, which, with thirty more that are nearly ready to start, will make one hundred and twenty melting furnaces, while the force of operations is increased to about three hundred. An idea of the enormous expense of running these great establishments may be obtained from the fact that this one consumes about one hundred and forty tons of coal a day, and in full operation consumes two hundred and forty crucibles a day, each crucible costing at present prices four dollars each, the total daily expense for these crucibles alone foots up the pleasant little sum of nine hundred and sixty dollars.[144]

40

The article continues that in addition to being the premier national supplier of "the finer qualities of cast steel, such as is used for edge tools, drills, etc." Hussey also:

> ...supplied New England with a large portion of the steel used here for the manufacture of cutlery for nearly three years, and the Cliff, North Cliff, Northwestern, Pontiac, Bay State, and other Lake Superior copper mines with drills and other mining tools, also the Denver and Colorado mines.[145]

In this respect, Hussey's steel enterprise overlapped directly with his earlier copper interests in the Lake Superior copper country and also presaged his later investment in western mines such as the 1871 silver mining claim certificate for Clear Creek County, Colorado[146] and elsewhere.

Just four years later, in 1868, a detailed description in *Railway Times* of the Hussey Wells steelworks in action indicates the enormous scale of the enterprise only nine years after production began:

> This firm began to manufacture cast steel in April 1859, with a force of about thirty hands and twelve small furnaces. To-day they employ upwards of 300 hands while their furnaces number one hundred and twenty.[147]

The *Railway Times* article divides the machinery and process descriptions into the melting room, the hammers, and the rolls. The melting room contained iron caps covering the below-floor furnaces, each 5-10 feet removed from the chimney flue attached to it. Removing the caps, workers would place crucibles into the fire below the floor. The melting process which produces steel from the pig iron proceeds:

> The process of melting and carbonizing the metal requires the closest attention and the most exact skill, hence the necessity of employing adepts. When that which was metal has had sufficient time in the opinion of the workman to be transformed into steel, he removes the cover from the surface and removing the crucible from its firey bed, proceeds cautiously and with great deliberation, to pour its molten contents into a cast-iron flask or mould...Great care is required in pouring the steel into these moulds, to prevent the molten metal from striking against the side, instead of directly upon the bottom of the mould. Should the steel touch the sides of the mould in its downward course, it is liable to "chill".

When cooled, clamps around the crucible were removed and steel ingots were released, varying in dimension and weight according to ultimate use. The smaller dimension ingot, 16 to 20 inches by 4 to 5 inches and weighing 50 to 150 pounds, proceeded to the hammers. The hammers were immense machines, at least 30 tons, tended by two men each, which operated an iron- headed wooden hammer to smash the heated steel to the exact dimensions required, from a thickness of ¼ inch to eight inches.

Much larger ingots, weighing five hundred to one thousand pounds each, were sent to the rolls to be fashioned into plates for the burgeoning market of boilers, especially for locomotives. The heated steel was rolled between two cylinders, eight feet long and about two feet in diameter into sheets between 1/4 and 3/4 inches in thickness, depending on how the workmen adjusted the upper roller. The size of each sheet was fifteen feet by five or six feet.[148]

Notable in these descriptions is that while brawn was abundantly required of the workers throughout their shifts, the operation also depended on their skill and judgment, not just in how to do the complex work, but when to move to the next step. That is, workers still had a key role in regulating the process and deciding when and how production proceeded. A mistake in timing or in processing, such as when pouring the molten steel from the crucibles into the molds, could ruin the whole batch. The array of end uses for this steel was vast, from tools for burgeoning western agriculture, to cutlery and razors, to railway engine boilers. The superiority of steel over iron in its relative strength allowed for much thinner metal that could withstand the boiler pressure. Tests done in Prussia that proved that

> ...the shell of the steel boiler was 33 per cent thinner than that of the wrought iron boiler tested.

Further tests for the Pennsylvania Railroad showed that the Hussey Wells steel was

> ...capable of sustaining 800 hydrostat pressure to the square inch..." which the author asserted showed "the immense superiority of steel over iron boilers.[149]

While Hussey hustled testimonials early in his steel career, he already had a good reputation in the financial world and was held in high regard throughout his life. Evidence of his reputation as a sound businessman surfaces throughout the middle of the 19th-century in the credit ledgers of R.G. Dun & Co, the predecessor of Dun & Bradstreet. An 1851 entry notes that in the Hussey & Hays pork company, Hussey had a $70,000 stake, Hayes $10,000.[3]

An October 1851 entry follows, noting " Hussey makes them v. good", suggesting the level of confidence held in Hussey as the senior partner.[150] An 1858 entry on C.G. Hussey & Co. reports: "V. wealthy – prime cr. - & of the highest standing".[151] Of the Hussey, Wells & Co. steelworks, an 1860 entry says " ...Mftg Steel Lately started this bus have build fine works, '& Co' are Thos M. Howe and Jas. M Cooper, both wealthy men....sound firm have unlimited cr." , followed in 1867 with a note that this is a "large bus very careful and worth 1½ to 2 millions (a1 & a1)".[152]

---

[3] For some perspective, note that Hussey's $70,000 stake conservatively represents over $2,000,000 in 2017 dollars, and that this is just his pork business, not even the copper by which he became truly wealthy, nor the steel wealth. Similarly, the 1867 R.G. Dun estimate of the value of Hussey, Wells & Co. steel company of $1,500,000 to $2,000,000 translates to $25,000,000 to $32,000,000 in today's dollars, with Hussey holding half the value.

Steel production before and after the establishment of Hussey, Wells & Co. reflects the explosive growth in steel production:

In 1860 the entire Pittsburgh steel sales for all firms was $880,000 on capital investment of $1,080,000, almost all inferior blister steel that was about to be superseded by Hussey's cast steel. In 1866, Hussey, Wells & Co alone sold $840,000 worth of cast steel.[153]

In 1867, when crucible steel production in the U.S was not yet separated from other older steel types, and the newer Bessemer-process steel was at a mere 2,676 tons, crucible and all other steel was at 16,964 tons.[154] By 1877 crucible steel production alone in the U.S. reached 40,430 net tons and only four years later in 1881 it had more than doubled again, to 89,430 tons.[155]

Metal-shaping factories across the country depended on cutting tools made of crucible steel through the 1920s, when electric steel furnaces replaced them. By 1879, *Iron Age* magazine showed eleven crucible steel manufacturers in Pittsburgh, including Hussey, Howe & Co., successor to Hussey, Wells & Co.:

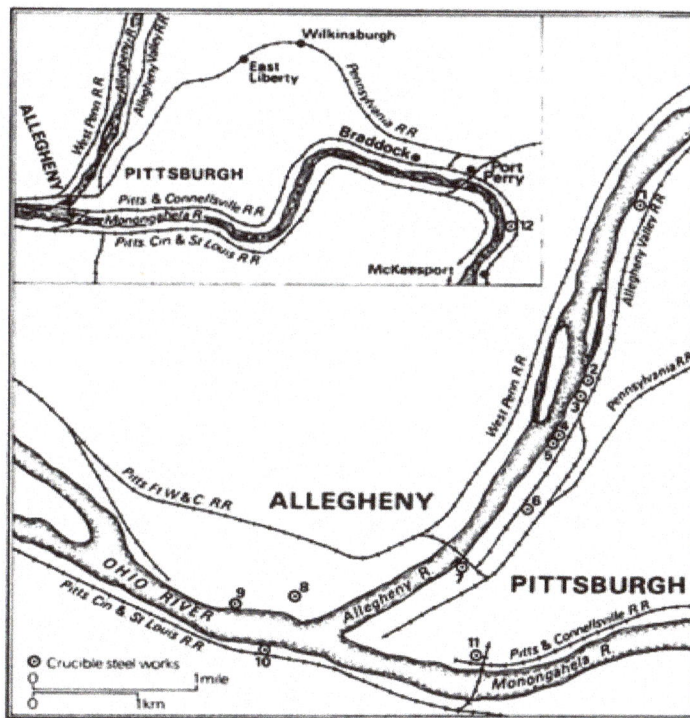

Map of Pittsburgh showing crucible steelworks

1. Crescent (Miller, Metcalf & Parkin)
2. Fort Pitt (John Graff)
3. Black Diamond (Park, Bro & Co)
4. Pittsburgh Steel Casting Co
5. Hussey, Binns & Co
6. Hussey, Howe & Co
7. Wayne (Brown & Co)
8. Nellis Agricultural (A. J. Nellis)
9. La Belle (Smith, Sutton & Co)
10. Sheffield (Singer, Nimick & Co)
11. Pittsburgh (Anderson & Co)
12. Pitt (Isaac Jones)

Source: *Iron Age* 23 (8 May 1879), p. 1.

Pittsburgh's eleven crucible steelworks in 1879[156]

After Wells left as a partner in Hussey, Wells & Co. to concentrate on his other interests, Hussey, Howe & Co. was incorporated on November 1, 1876, with Hussey's partner both in the steelworks and from as far back as the Cliff mine, General Thomas Marshall Howe, now assuming Wells' position in the firm name. As with the copper mine, Howe's involvement was critical as a financial backer, but he was not actively involved in either the copper or steel enterprises.[157]

According to the newspaper announcement of the new firm, Hussey's thirty- two-year-old son, Christopher Curtis Hussey, had already been a partner in Hussey, Wells & Co.:

DISSOLUTION.

———

The copartnership heretofore existing under the firm name of HUSSEY, WELLS & CO. is this day dissolved, Calvin Wells and the estate of James M. Cooper, deceased, retiring.
The business of the late firm will be settled by the surviving partners.
C. G. HUSSEY,
THOMAS M. HOWE,
CALVIN WELLS,
C. CURTIS HUSSEY,
A. H. MILLER,
J. MASLIN COOPER, } Executors of Jas. M. Cooper, dec'd.
Pittsburgh, November 1, 1876.

———

THE REMAINING PARTNERS, UNDER the firm name of HUSSEY, HOWE & CO., will continue the Steel business heretofore conducted by the late firm of Hussey, Wells & Co.
HUSSEY, HOWE & CO.
Pittsburgh, November 1, 1876.   MWF

Notice of Hussey, Wells & Co. transition to Hussey, Howe & Co. , 1876 [158]

By the 1880s, Hussey's steelworks had burgeoned proportionally to the growth of the crucible steel industry itself. Describing his visit to Hussey, Howe & Co. on July 17, 1882, a Sheffield, England steel man, Robert A Hadfield's description of the Hussey steelworks was decidedly less breathlessly admiring than that of the 1868 *Boston Commercial Bulletin* report correspondent of nearly twenty years earlier. The workforce was tripled from the 1868 report but he offers pungent detail about the operation of the plant:

> ....Employ 900 men, 12,000 tons per anum, 2 Siemens open hearth furnaces, also gas pot holes. Pots (carry 90 lbs. & more), last 6 rounds, saw some daubed where worn and used again....Very hot day, men nearly naked & sweating away. Pulling 90 lb. pots out of the whole like fun. Head puller earning $12 day (L2!) Puller out $5. No wonder men are tempted to go to the states....

Hadfield was also not impressed with the quality of the steel and pulled aside an English emigrant, George Capper who was working as a hammer foreman, who reported that:

> ... 'It lacks the body and had not the quality of good English steel, it stands too much heat.' Also said they put such common stuff in the pot no wonder the quality was poor...

Hadfield continues:

> These works are the oldest steelworks in Pittsburgh. Cannot say that their warehouse and stock is imposing.[159]

Neither the foreman's comments nor Hadfield's observation seem consistent with other assessments of the quality of American crucible steel and its success in supplanting British tool steel. The two Englishmen may have been inspired by a bit of British chauvinism.

After an abortive effort in a new venture to produce steel by the Bessemer process, described in the following section, C.G. Hussey finally left the steel business entirely when the steelworks he had founded as Hussey, Wells & Co in 1858 became Howe, Brown & Co in 1888. He was eight-seven years old and five years from his death when he sold out to the widow and son-in-law of his old partner in multiple ventures, Thomas M. Howe:

Notice of 1888 sale of the Hussey share of Hussey, Howe & Co. to Mary H. Howe, widow of Thomas M. Howe[160]

In 1900 most of the crucible steel companies merged to form the Crucible Steel Company of America, foreshadowing the following year's consolidation in the Bessemer steel production, which became J.P. Morgan's United States Steel Corporation. The three largest crucible firms to join were Howe, Brown, and Company, Sanderson Brothers, and Park Brothers, as well as ten smaller companies:

- Aliquippa Steel Company, several miles north of Pittsburgh on the Ohio River
- Anderson, DuPuy and Company
- Beaver Falls Steel Works
- Burgess Steel and Iron Works
- Crescent Steel of Pittsburgh
- Cumberland Steel and Tin Plate Company
- Isaac Jones' Pittsburgh Steel Works (later Anderson, Deputy and Company)
- LaBelle Steel Company
- Singer, Nimick and Company of Pittsburgh
- Spaulding and Jennings Company

The Crucible Steel Company continued to supply crucible steel for more than a century until entering Chapter 11 receivership in 2009.[161] As with his copper smelting and rolling mill, Hussey had generated a steel corporation built to last.

Crucible Steel and Bessemer Steel

Before he left the steel business in 1888, C.G. Hussey and his son Christopher C. Hussey and several other partners made an abortive foray into a newer process for making steel, the Bessemer process. Bessemer developed later than the crucible process and was the foundation for the Carnegie steel empire. However, Hussey's 1879-1883 Bessemer venture was not his first chance at Bessemer. At the very dawn of the Bessemer age, he had been given the chance to add Bessemer steel to his burgeoning crucible steel business.

In 1862, with Hussey, Wells & Co. well-established as the first major crucible steel maker in the United States, Hussey went to England to investigate first-hand the steel making of Sheffield, whose monopoly on crucible steel market in America was about to be supplanted by the efforts of himself and other aspiring Pittsburgh steel makers.

On this visit he was offered a revolutionary new way to make steel, the Bessemer process, for use in America. He turned it down, believing that the process was not yet perfected.[162] This appears to be a rare case in which Hussey did not immediately grasp the importance of an emerging technology, as steel produced by the Bessemer process soon overtook the crucible steel numbers. Once the Bessemer process gained momentum, the growth of steel production using that process was exponential and vastly outpaced the crucible steel process. Since Hussey was only two years into producing steel at all, his reluctance to adopt yet another direction may be understandable. Instead, the first American manufacturer of Bessemer steel in the United States was Captain Eben B. Ward in Detroit in 1864[163] And it was Andrew Carnegie whose titanic success, starting in the mid-1870s, was based on Bessemer steel.

Crucible steel and Bessemer steel coexisted well into the next century because of the different uses to which they were particularly suited. As crucible tool steel differed in production method, quality, cost, and use from blister and shear steel, so too did Bessemer steel differ from crucible steel. Bessemer is best for where cheapness and quantity matter more than quality but with quality near that of tool steel. Bessemer-produced steel was used for locomotive rails and steel framing of modern buildings, which explains the explosive growth in production in the late 19th-century, replacing wrought iron. For uses requiring a finer and harder grade of steel, such as boilers in steam engines, manufacturing machinery, or cutting tools, crucible steel remained the required product.[164] The two types of steel did not really directly compete and crucible steel was only supplanted as tool steel in the 20th century by electric-arc steel production, as foreseen in a 1917 report on iron and steel as the era of crucible steel was coming to a close:

> Even today the crucible process is holding its own where quality is the main consideration. It is the method by which practically all of the tool, automobile, and other specialty steels of today are manufactured and can hardly be given too high a rating. The newly devised electric furnace process is the only possible competitor in sight.[165]

Despite their different uses, there was some overlap between crucible and Bessemer steel, as "the most expensive grades [i.e. crucible] were bought only after a thorough search for cheaper alternatives [i.e., Bessemer]"[166] That is, if Bessemer could do the job, take Bessemer; otherwise pay for crucible. In any case, Bessemer- produced steel fueled the immense growth in steel production that we associate with Andrew Carnegie and which quickly supplanted crucible steel as the largest sector of steel manufacturing. In 1869, U.S. Bessemer steel production was 10,714 tons and all other steel (including crucible) was 19,643 tons. By 1880, Bessemer production was at 1,074,262 tons and crucible at 64,664 tons.[167] So, even though crucible steel production continued to grow rapidly in the Bessemer era, it was utterly dwarfed by the new process.

Two men in the 1840s and 1850s independently and nearly simultaneously had discovered this new and cheaper way to make steel: William Kelly in Missouri, in 1847 and Henry Bessemer in the United Kingdom, in 1855. Kelly probably preceded Bessemer and he held a U.S. patent, which he only took out when he heard about Bessemer doing the same in England.[168] However, for a variety of reasons related to business skills, machinery inadequacies and personality, Kelly did not end up being the main player in this new process.[169] The first successful American Bessemer works was built by Alexander Lyman Holley for Corning, Winslow, and Company of Troy, New York, in 1865, using the Kelly patents. Still, Holley realized that success in the United States required the reconciliation of the various competing Kelly and Bessemer patents. This transpired with the founding, in 1866, of the Pneumatic Steel Company to hold those patents and license them to others.

Holley continued to play a critical role in establishing Bessemer works, including Andrew Carnegie's first Bessemer works, the Edgar Thomson Steelworks in 1872.[170]

The Bessemer process, as perfected, included three key elements. First, and most critically, Bessemer and Kelly realized, against intuition, that with a blast of cold air into the molten pig iron, oxygen would unite with the carbon and other impurities such as sulfur and in an explosive conflagration leave a purer iron.[171]

With the right amount of carbon left in, the result is steel. Removing the precise amount of carbon to leave the desired percentage was difficult. This second technical difficulty was solved by Robert F. Mushet. Instead of trying to gauge when enough of the carbon had been burnt out to meet the steel requirements, he fired the steel until all the carbon was gone, then added back in the required amount, thus improving the accuracy of the mixture.[172]

Finally, Bessemer himself invented the tilting converter and ladle that transferred the molten steel to the molds. The steel could now be poured slowly and carefully into the molds to maintain the uniformity of the steel.[173]

Pittsburgh Bessemer Steel Corporation

When perfected, the Bessemer process became the standard for mass- produced steel. Although he had earlier passed on the Bessemer process, C.G. Hussey's last act in steel was to partner with five other investors to create the Pittsburgh Bessemer Steel Corporation (PBSC) to build the Pittsburgh Bessemer Steelworks (PBSW), incorporated October 21, 1879, and known also as the Homestead Steelworks. With a capital investment of $250,000, the six partners were William G. Park of the Park Brothers & Co., Curtis G. and Christopher C. Hussey of Hussey, Howe & Co, William H. Singer, of Singer, Nimick & Co., each with five shares at $10,000 each, Reuben Miller of Crescent Steelworks and William Clark of Solar Iron and Steelworks with four shares each, and Andrew Kloman with two shares.[174]

Andrew Kloman was the key player among the founders because of his technical skills and his experience with their major competitor, Andrew Carnegie. A former partner of Carnegie both in the giant Lucy furnace, the leading iron- producing blast furnace in country, and the Edgar Thomson steelworks, which he had worked with Holley to create in 1872, Kloman had a bone to pick with Carnegie. Carnegie had forced him out of the Edgar Thomson works because he was using his profits there to invest in ventures without consulting Carnegie, which Carnegie considered both ill-advised and disloyal.[175]

Kloman and Holley were critical to the success of Homestead because the PBSC founders were not part of the Bessemer Steel Company, Ltd., the 1877 successor to the Pneumatic Steel Company, the steel manufacturers' consortium which still held the Bessemer patents and with which Holley remained associated. Through the Bessemer Steel Company. Ltd., this pool of steel manufacturers could either deny use of patents or charge a licensing fee to non-members. While Kloman's association with the emerging

PBSW was direct, Holley's was less clear. The technical details of the Homestead design, as well as contemporary accounts, suggest that Holley had a hand in creating the Homestead works without trespassing on the Bessemer patents of which he was a guardian as a member of the Bessemer Steel Company, Ltd.[176]

Let loose by Carnegie and with his lease on his own Superior Mill had having run out in 1879, Kloman began anew by building himself a mill in Homestead.

Simultaneously, PBSC built its adjoining converting works and blooming mill, construction of which was supervised by Kloman. The plan was for Kloman to take for his own production needs any excess steel that PBSC produced.

Within fifteen months, Homestead was up and running, producing its first steel On March 19, 1881.[177] However, Kloman died suddenly and PBSC bought his unfinished mill.[178] Kloman's finishing mill was designed to produce 50,000 tons of steel rails and 30,000 tons of structural steel, using the steel produced by the original PBSC's works. While not on the scale of Carnegie, who in 1879 produced 100,094 tons of the total Bessemer output of 123,303,[179] this was a substantial output for the first major competitor to Carnegie. By the fall, Homestead was already churning out 200 tons of rails a day and had an order for 15,000 tons.[180] For the first time, Carnegie's Edgar Thomson works had serious competition and Homestead as the second major U.S. producer of Bessemer steel promised to be a threat.

No doubt the crucible steelmakers who founded Homestead were eager to get into the larger Bessemer market. However, Homestead was founded, in part, because of yet another way the crucible and Bessemer steel companies had overlapping complementary needs despite mostly competing in different markets. By this time, crucible steel makers were using cheaper steel in place of pig iron to produce their high-grade steel. Carnegie had been supplying his excess Bessemer steel as raw material to Hussey and other tool steel makers in the economically depressed late '70s but cut them off in 1879 as the economy improved and he could go back to producing exclusively for rails and construction.[181] The Homestead consortium would free the crucible steel makers from the vagaries of Carnegie's supply. Their new plant was to be the answer to the crucible steel makers need for a steady supply of raw material for production of their special type of steel, as well as a direct competitor to Carnegie for rails and other Bessemer steel.

Despite the successful start, the Homestead project soon faltered through a combination of a labor problems and a faltering economy. Not long after going into full production in the fall of 1881, the workers threatened to strike at a critical moment in production. Co-owner and manager William Clark initially bowed to them, but at the end of the year he demanded that all workers sign an agreement renouncing their right to unionize and leaving their unions (most were Amalgamated Association of Iron and Steel Workers – AAISW – the increasingly powerful union founded in 1875 from three previous metalworker unions). They refused and were locked out.

Throughout 1882 labor disputes wracked the Homestead works. When the

AAISW threatened to strike at other works owned by the partners, the Homestead management capitulated, withdrawing the original demand and substituting one that required three days' notice for a strike, but would not budge on reduced wages. The union rebuffed this offer, and the strike continued. It was finally settled in March 1882, and resulted in Clark's resignation as superintendent.

Invigorated by their victory, the Homestead workers immediately demanded a raise and went on a strike that lasted four months. They were joined by all other unionized ironworkers. Although the strike ended in failure in September, the labor troubles combined with the depressed prices for steel spooked the Homestead owners.[182] They were particularly worried at the prospect of their respective mills elsewhere being hurt by the ongoing problems, a threat which had been made explicit early in March by the AAISW[183] and likely contributed to the settlement that had driven Clark out earlier in 1882. Whether a direct result of the March AAISW threat or not, labor strife spread to Hussey, Howe & Co. in May. In response, the Husseys acceded to the AAISW demand to go back to the rate of $6 per ton, the rate up until two years previous.[184]

The Pittsburgh Bessemer Steel Corporation owners had had enough. They approached Carnegie and offered to sell. Carnegie accepted, agreeing to reimburse them for their initial investment of $250,000, but no more. Homestead passed to him in October 1883.[185] Carnegie had offered all the owners a choice of cash or shares but only one Homestead owner accepted shares, William H. Singer. Instead of taking his $50,000 investment in cash, he received shares that were worth $8 million barely fifteen years later[186] when Carnegie sold to J.P. Morgan for the founding of U.S. Steel. Not surprisingly, Singer had a presence in the new company that ran Homestead, Carnegie, Phipps & Co. However, C. G. Hussey's son Christopher Hussey also maintained a toehold in management as one of the directors:

> The Pittsburgh Bessemer Steelworks at Homestead have not been entirely swallowed by Carnegie Bros & Co., although two members of that firm hold an interest in the plant. The Pittsburgh company is now managed by W.H. Singer, Henry Phipps, Jr., C.C. Hussey, H.M. Curry, and H.P. Smith. Mr. Singer is the chairman and Mr. Smith secretary.[187]

Carnegie Brothers & Co. had been formed in 1881 to consolidate various Carnegie enterprises, including the Lucy Furnaces and the Edgar Thomson Steelworks, but in fact was not consolidated with Carnegie, Phipps & Co. until 1892 with the formation of the Carnegie Steel Corporation. [188]

As in his 1862 rejection of the Bessemer process, so too Hussey faltered in creating a successful Bessemer steelworks, though not without putting a scare into Andrew Carnegie, who within four years of the founding of the Pittsburgh Bessemer Steel Corporation founding had absorbed the formidable competition of the Homestead works. The inclusion of Christopher Hussey in the new management hints at the likelihood that he, not the elderly Curtis Hussey, was the key Hussey player in decisions related to the

Pittsburgh Bessemer Steel Corporation.

Labor and Steelmaking

The founding of Homestead provides a wealth of insight into the rivalries, shifting alliances, and personalities of the Pittsburgh steel barons of the era as the Carnegie juggernaut gained momentum. And no recounting of 19th-century steel manufacturing would be complete without understanding the contemporary labor movement in Pittsburgh as labor fought for influence when demand for their old craft skills was on the wane in modern more technically efficient factories. In the end, Carnegie prevailed over his competitors and labor was crushed, but the story of the short-lived Pittsburgh Bessemer Steelworks in 1878-1883 set the stage for these momentous events.[4]

Steelmakers explicitly saw the Bessemer process as aiding their push for efficiency, technological change, and higher profits. They also considered the Bessemer process an ally in expanding management power and weakening worker and union power. Bessemer steel initially competed with wrought iron, previously the main metal for structures and rails. The critical step in creating wrought iron from pig iron was "puddling", in which the molten pig iron was heated to drive out impurities. The men handling this job, the puddlers, depended on skills learned at length and by experience to know exactly what to do and when. The science behind the process was little understood. This gave the puddlers power not only over their pay, but also over the entire steel-making process. Like their predecessors in England who had created steel through the old cementation process, these were proud men who valued their skills, expected their worth to be rewarded with a decent living, and even determined the amount of output, for example, how many "burns" they would do in a shift. They considered the value of their work as objectively "worth" a decent living.

These attitudes rankled the owners. The owners and their managers were deeply committed to modern industrialization that embraced technological changes and division of labor in ways that reduced the need for skilled labor and produced more uniform and predictable output. Moreover, they saw the cost of labor as being simply another expense, which should be directly tied to the price they could fetch for the finished product.[189]

Even as their power as skilled craftsmen waned, the steelworkers responded with the terminology of free men which they thought distinguished them from more subservient Europeans, a view of freedom that had been explicitly expressed and triumphantly achieved in the recent Civil War. For example, Abram Hewitt, the first American to experiment with Bessemer and open hearth and a leading ideologue of the need for engineers and managers to control the process, said that "I do not say it in derogation [of the worker]. But it is for the master to do the thinking." This infuriated the workers, Sons of Vulcans, who considered this "an assault against the moral standing of

---

[4] The Homestead steelworks, founded by Pittsburgh Bessemer Steel Corporation and taken over by Carnegie in 1883, went on to notoriety as the site of one of the most momentous labor incidents in American history, the Homestead strike of 1892, in which Carnegie once and for all crushed the union and set the tone for the next several decades of labor movement suppression.

the union and a base calumny upon...free American citizens." [190] This sentiment extended beyond the labor movement. The *New York Times* in 1869 asserted that:

> ...there is gradually developing at the North a system of slavery as absolute if not as degrading as that which lately prevailed in the South. The only difference is that there agriculture was the field, landed proprietors were the masters, and Negroes were the slaves; while in the North manufactures is the field, manufacturing capitalists threaten to be the masters, and it is the white laborers who are to be the slaves.

Tying this developing condition to England, as well, the article asserts that

> ...the inevitable tendency of the industrial North is to reduce the laboring class is to the same condition of absolute dependency, in which 22,000,000 of the English manufacturing and agricultural laborers now struggle.[191]

This sentiment had not abated when in 1882 a striking worker at the Homestead works while it was still under control of the original owners exhorted his comrades:

> Just think of it, my fellow workmen, living in a land where not twenty years ago we had a war against slavery, in which many of our brave citizens lost their lives, wives were made widows and children orphans; in a land where freedom and independence was proclaimed, that we, as employees of Pittsburgh Bessemer Steelworks, would go in our right minds and sober senses and sign away our rights as free-born American citizens.[192]

It was in this context that labor had made an explicit bid for political power in Pittsburgh in the years 1865-1868. An independent Labor Party and a stew of various Republican and Democratic factions, all claiming to be pro-worker, and engaging in a constant kaleidoscopic reconfiguration of alliances, jockeyed for power.[193] In the end, the Republicans prevailed by tying anyone voting Democratic or Labor Reform as either KKK, or subversive Catholics, so that "...in the industrial North after the Civil War, workers and leaders were under enormous pressure to vote as they had shot." The result was the machine GOP politician Christopher L Magee, who "ultimately succeeding in marketing his political machine as the genuine voice of Pittsburgh's workers." [194] The fight moved to the factory floor as labor power at the ballot box was coopted and neutered.

This ideological struggle – the rights of the manufacturers to control all details of their businesses vs. the rights of workers as free men – was the hallmark of the 1870s in Pittsburgh. Manufacturers continued to modernize and rationalize their plants and workers continued to organize in the mills.

There is no evidence that C.G. Hussey was any more sympathetic to labor than other industrialists. However, there were nuances in how steel men treated their workers, for practical if not necessarily humanitarian reasons. Homestead Superintendent (and part owner of Pittsburgh Bessemer Steel Corporation) William

Clark, for example, was far more rigid and antagonistic toward his workers than was his counterpart Captain William R. Jones at Carnegie's Edgar Thomson works. Jones was no less a foe of organized labor, but he knew how to fraternize with and support his workers. Jones, for example, arranged to have the Edgar Thomson works help his men to buy houses.[195]

The problems at Homestead may indicate that Hussey was no longer as active as he had been in his other ventures. Judging by his temperament and based on his long experience with his copper and crucible steel businesses, he certainly had the capacity to have handled the labor issue better. His successful track record of hiring managers suggests more men like William Jones and fewer like William Clark.

Moreover, he had repeatedly shown the nerve to make substantial investments at difficult times and see them through. The financial difficulties that, with the labor problems, plagued Homestead and drove the investors to bail out so soon do not seem characteristic of the Hussey of the 1840s and 1850s.

Whether or not a more actively engaged C. G. Hussey might have saved the Pittsburgh Bessemer Steel Corporation, he was by this time much less involved in his businesses. To be sure, in the case of the PBSC, the Hussey interest constituted only one-sixth of the group of investors, and he was 80 when Carnegie bought them all out. Moreover, his son, Christopher Hussey, was clearly assuming the role for which he had been groomed. At the time of the PBSC sale it was Christopher, who with four of the five other original investors -- W. H. Singer, Reuben Miller, W.G. Park, and Wm. Clark -- were listed as "Managers" in the Pittsburgh Bessemer Steel Corporation correspondence with Andrew Carnegie about the sale of Homestead.[196]

Christopher Hussey's involvement in steel was not limited to Hussey, Wells & Co. (Hussey, Howe & Co. from 1876) and the Pittsburgh Bessemer Steel Corporation. In 1874 Christopher Hussey had founded the firm of Hussey & Binns, later called Hussey-Binns Shovel Co., with his cousin and brother-in-law Edward Binns.[5] If not directly financed by C.G. Hussey, this new venture by a pair of 30-year-old cousins surely owed much to the wealth flowing from C.G. Hussey.

Another sign of Christopher Hussey's growing role was that when the British steel man Robert A. Hadfield visited the Hussey, Howe & Co. steelworks in July 1882, as previously described, he notes that it was "Mr. Hussey Jnr" who met with him. Commonwealth of Pennsylvania corporate records also show Christopher's increased direct role in the corporate leadership of C.G Hussey's original steel operation. In the 1882 Pennsylvania document that renewed the 1880 limited partnership of Hussey,

---

[5] The genealogy gets a little complicated here: Christopher Curtis Hussey and Edward Binns were cousins, Binns being the son of C.G. Hussey's sister Anna McPherson Hussey Binns. However, Edward Binns married another first cousin, Anna Hussey, sister of Christopher and daughter of C.G. Hussey.

Howe & Co, C. Curtis Hussey (Christopher Curtis Hussey) was listed as chairman, with James W. Brown serving as Secretary and Treasurer. The firm was capitalized at $1 million, with Mary A. Howe, the widow of Thomas M. Howe, owning $496,000, C.G. Hussey with $333,000, C .Curtis Hussey with $167,000, and Brown with $4,000[197]. James Brown was married to Clara Howe, daughter of Mary and Thomas Howe.[198]

The capitalization figure was the same in 1880, 1885, and 1888 and likely does not reflect the actual value, especially considering the previously cited R.D. Dun report that as early as 1867 estimated the value as $1,500, 000 to $2,000,000. However, it does indicate that the Howe family, with Brown's small share, owned half of the corporation and that C.G. Hussey had ceded 1/3 of his ½ half share of the company to Christopher. Christopher's obituary in 1884 also noted that he was chairman of Hussey, Howe & Co.[199] With his son's premature death in 1884, C.G. Hussey resumed direct control of Hussey, Howe, & Co. as chairman when the three-year term of the partnership came up for renewal in 1885, while Christopher's wife Harriet assumed her late husband's role as a "manager" but not an officer.[200] When the partnership came up again for renewal in 1888, the long- expected generational transition of leadership in Hussey, Howe & Co. was abandoned when C.G Hussey and Harriet Hussey sold their shares to Mary Anne Howe.[201]

For the five final years of his long life, C.G Hussey no longer had a direct role in steel. With both his son and his nephew, Christopher Curtis Hussey and Edward Binns, dead at early ages (1884 and 1877 respectively), their steel company, the Hussey-Binns Shovel Co. was the only steel business left in the Hussey family. Of C.G. Hussey's three male grandsons, Christopher's son, the second Curtis Grubb Hussey, never played an active role in the Hussey businesses and, like so many Hussey men, died prematurely in 1924, while visiting his sister in Cape Town, South Africa.

Edward Binns' sons, Edward Hussey Binns and Ralph Holden Binns, were raised by C.G. and Rebecca Hussey at their Shadyside estate in Pittsburgh. All three grandsons inherited the C.G. Hussey & Co copper interests at C.G. Hussey's death.

Edward Hussey Binns ran C.G. Hussey & Co. until losing it in the Depression, while Ralph Holden Binns ran Hussey-Binns Shovel Co., which went bankrupt in 1918 and was sold to Universal Steel, ending the sixty-year run of the Husseys and steel.[202]

Since the 1860s Hussey had played an increasingly active role in a wide variety of philanthropic activities in Pittsburgh and elsewhere. These remained a focus even in his last years.

Philanthropy

C.G. Hussey's interests extended well beyond his industrial and commercial endeavors, as disparate and complex as these were. In the second half of his life, Hussey supported a wide range of philanthropic endeavors, primarily educational, and mostly with a focus on the advancement of women or African Americans. All were consistent with his activist Quaker upbringing. Most entailed long-term financial support over decades. Often, he was a founder or early leader. There is less evidence that he played an active role in governance or management of these institutions, but there is some evidence of his strong opinions about who should be running the institutions he supported, particularly with respect to the role of women.

Contemporary biographical accounts asserted that Hussey was an active supporter of many progressive social and educational causes of the era. Typical is this paragraph:

> Dr. CG Hussey was a staunch Quaker who contributed heavily to the causes of Women's Suffrage, Anti-Slavery and Temperance. He founded several schools for girls and women's colleges throughout the US and Mexico. One of his business partners founded the first African American college in America and was a documented leader and financier of the Underground Railroad in the Pittsburgh area. [203]

C.G. Hussey at age eight-two in 1884 [204]

Education

Several Hussey projects supported both education and women, two of his major philanthropic interests. One of the most successful and innovative was the Pittsburgh School of Design for Women, founded in 1865, which ceased independent existence in 1905. This school was modeled on the Philadelphia School of Design for Women, founded in 1848. Similar schools appeared in Boston, New York, and Cincinnati.[205] Design schools for women met a complementary variety of needs, both practical and high-minded. Mid 19th-century industrialists sought to apply design standards to their manufactured goods to gain competitive advantage, as described by historian Britta Christina Dwyer:

> As the application of artistic design to manufactured goods became important to the marketing of a product, the word design was used to identify decorative treatments applied to the form and surface of a product, such as a fabric, a wallpaper, a utilitarian appliance, or machine. Better design products, the mercantilists argued, could be accomplished by extending the activity of schools of art into the manufacturing sphere.[206]

Such a forward-looking marketing strategy fit well with Hussey's business sense. But socially conscious industrialists like Hussey also supported the education of women in principle. Such men recognized the growing numbers of women who were single or heads of household and found synergy that was useful for their businesses in providing options other than poorly paid household domestic service jobs or home piecework such as sewing. The design schools also aligned with the 19th-century sensibility that artistic endeavors were particularly aligned with the "women's sphere." Moreover, once trained, the "respectable" women graduates could work at home, free from the contamination of the office or factory.[207] The Pittsburgh School of Design served mostly middle or lower middle-class women. The students were mostly daughters of craftsmen.[208]

Thomas W. Braidwood was founder of the Philadelphia school, and he sought out Hussey for the first Branch School[209]. Mary J. Grieg served as Head Teacher until 1867 when she married Nicholas Veeder, a close associate of Hussey's in many businesses and one of three executors named in Hussey's 1889 will, although Veeder did not serve as executor, dying in 1891.[6] Braidwood served as the non- resident principal, visiting on a

---

[6] Nicholas Veeder, while not a peer of Hussey like Howe or Wells, was another example of a man Hussey found useful and reliable very early on and who shows up repeatedly throughout Hussey's life in many different endeavors and capacities. In addition to marrying the principal of the Pittsburgh School of Design for Women, Veeder shows up as early as 1850 as secretary to Hussey's Aztec Mining Co., as well as an officer in other Hussey ventures such as Cumberland Oil Co. and Hussey Oil Co. (both founded in 1866). He is identified as having been an accountant in Hussey's business when he was secretary to the original Observatory board before it was absorbed by the Western University of Pennsylvania in 1865, and he continued as secretary to the Observatory Committee of the university's Board of Trustees. He was administrator of the estate of C.G. Hussey's younger brother, Joseph Hussey, at Joseph's death in 1883. In a strong statement of Hussey confidence in Veeder, he was named as one of three executors of C.G.'s 1889 will and guardian of Hussey's granddaughter Mary Guthrie, although he died before Hussey and was replaced by Hussey's grandson Edward Hussey Binns. The will also specified that Veeder was to receive a 1/6 share in the C.G Hussey & Co copper business as compensation for being general manager (the same

regular basis.[210] The founders put up $7-8000 and the school opened on February 1, 1865, on the third floor of the Phelan Building on Fifth Street, with Hussey as president.

The curriculum was extensive, designed for three or four years of matriculation, although the first nine students only graduated in 1872.[211] The curriculum included:

> ...geometry, perspective, drawing, drawing and shading from casts of architectural ornament, busts, physical anatomy, then practical subjects like applied design, decorative painting (pottery), wood engraving, lithography.[212]

An 1874 newspaper report about the prizes awarded at the annual exhibition of artwork confirms the breadth of the studies, citing prizes for geometry, perspectives, elementary outlines, figures in outline, landscapes in pencil, sepia, or color, India ink flowers, watercolor flowers and from nature, diagrams in color, drawing from geometrical figures, busts, details from figure, anatomical and full length figures, studies in oil, figures and groups in oil, ornament from cast, and original ornamental designs.[213] In 1903, near the end of its existence, the school was still offering prizes for fewer, but similar, art categories, as well as for work by students in Saturday classes.[214]

1878 medal awarded to Bertha Doerflinger for oil painting.[215]

Hussey's response to a change in the Head Teacher position points to his strong feelings about women in leadership positions. When Mary Greig left the position to marry Veeder, Esther K. Hayhurst succeeded as Head Teacher. However, Hayhurst in turn left in 1867 and was succeeded by Hugh Newell.[216] This resulted in Hussey resigning as president because "the election of a man to the management of an institution founded expressly for the benefit of women was contrary to his sense of right".[217]

---

deal applied to Dravo), although the business was technically divided in thirds among the three grandsons.

Braidwood resigned as Principal in 1872 and PSDW formally split from the parent Philadelphia school, gradually turning from the mercantilist angle more explicitly to women's artistic interests.[218] However, Hussey continued to serve on the board and support the school until his death.[219] In 1884, the school moved to the top floor of the YMCA at 7th and Penn, at the instigation of William Thaw, who became the key supporter of the school in its later years.[220]

Circa 1900-1915 postcard of the Central YMCA at 7th & Penn. The Pittsburgh School of Design for Women occupied the top floor from 1884 until 1904[221]

The end came in 1904 when the YMCA reclaimed the top floor. The school did not lack backers with money. At the end the board included, Edward B. Alsop, with a large fortune, Richard Mellon, Henry Clay Frick, and Henry Phipps. However, there was no endowment.[222] The board simply made up the deficit each year. Dwyer believes that the later board members were more perfunctory, far removed from the early mercantilist strain that had been a primary motivation for founding the school. While the founders may have been supportive of the transition to a more purely art school, their successors may not have been as devoted once the original mercantilist purpose was lost.[223] Moreover, at least some of the last trustees may well have just been carrying on out of familial duty rather than real support. Alsop was Hussey's son-in-law and another trustee, Ralph Holden Binns, was his grandson, whom Hussey had raised after the early deaths of Hussey's daughter Anna Hussey Binns and her husband Edward Binns.

The school closed on June 24, 1904. The following July, the board donated all school properties to Pennsylvania College for Women (now Chatham University, and where Hussey had also been a trustee). In 1913, that college passed any remnants to its Alumnae Association, which in turn passed it on to the University of Pittsburgh according to an Alumni Association document of 1921-2.[224].

In addition to the Pittsburgh School of Design and the Pennsylvania College for Women, Hussey had a hand in several other schools for women. The most exotic was the Hussey School for Girls in Matamoros, Tamaulipas state, Mexico, across from Brownsville, Texas. This school was founded in 1872 by Quaker missionaries Samuel Purdie and his wife, Gulielma, as an adjunct to the church mission they founded there.[225] Purdie also printed a monthly missionary tract in Spanish and other religious tracts. The mission was sponsored by the American Friends Board of Missions and supported primarily by Indiana Friends chapter.[226] and had connections as well with Guilford College in North Carolina, which provided many of the teachers.[227]

Hussey became associated with this venture in 1885, when Purdie raised $4000 to create a boarding school to complement the day school.[228] Hussey provided $3100 of that amount to erect the building across the plaza from the church. He later donated an additional $5000, and a final $5000 bequest in his will.

Opening in 1886, the boarding school housed twelve girls and the teachers, who also taught the day students, numbering around 100. The school became the responsibility of the Women's Foreign Missionary Association of the Indiana Yearly Meeting. As with the Pittsburgh School of Design for Women, from its start as the Hussey Institute, women had played the major roles as teachers and administrators, including Julia L. Ballinger, who had been associated with the school since 1883 and who had served as principal for some of that time.

In 1892 the school was expanded so that the day students studied in a separate adjoining building and the original Hussey Institute building housed the boarders only. At its peak in the early 20th century the school served 30 boarders and around 180 in the day school. As many as 1000 students studied at the Hussey Institute over the course of its history.[229] A few boys in the lower grades attended as day students, but the school remained primarily for girls.[230]

The C. G. Hussey School for Girls.   Plaza de la Libertad, Matamoros, Mexico.

Hussey School for Girls in Matamoros, Mexico, 1908 [231]

Hussey had never completely cut his ties with Indiana more than half a century earlier, so he may have been solicited by his fellow Quakers from that state who were supporting Purdie's Matamoras school. The school ceased independent existence in 1917 when the Mexican revolution led to state ownership of all church schools.[232]

Hussey's interest in expanding educational opportunities for those historically excluded was not limited to women. Hussey's old friend and investor in the Cliff Mine, Charles Avery, received a charter for the Allegheny Institute and Mission Church (later Avery College) on March 20, 1849 as "...a college for the education of colored Americans, in the various branches of sciences, literature, and ancient and modern languages....".[233]

While Oberlin College had been the first American college to admin Black students in 1835, the little-remembered Avery College was the first college exclusively for Black students.[234] Both male and females were to be admitted and Avery donated land worth $5,000 and $10,000 for the construction of a building.[235] Significantly, the charter specified that only one-third of the trustees would be white[236] and three of its four presidents were African American. It survived as a college barely more than twenty years. Near the end of its existence, under the presidency of its most successful leader, the Rev. Henry Highland Garnet, a detailed account in 1868 lists four faculty (two men, two women) teaching a rigorous academic curriculum for which the students paid $2 per semester, three semesters per year.[237] Garnet's 1870 resignation marked the effective end of the college, although it struggled on under a successor who was never named president, until closing for good in 1873.[238]

The rise and fall of the first historically Black college in America was deeply

60

influenced by the complex threads of the antebellum anti-slavery movement and the conflicts over educational policy for the newly freed slaves in the early Reconstruction era. Chief among the ideological struggles that eventually doomed Avery College were views of African re-colonization, integration vs. single-race education, academic vs. vocational education, and white vs. Black control of educational resources.

Unfortunately for Avery College, Avery himself died in 1858. He left a large fortune, estimated at $350,000 to $400,000, primarily for education of Blacks, but the distribution of that estate fell to executors, two out of three of whom were not as supportive of many of the original aims of the college. Avery College received nothing from the 1866 disbursement of the Avery estate.[239]

Hussey stepped in at a critical moment when Avery died in 1858. He became president of the board of trustees and served until the demise of the school, but there is little evidence that he played a significant role in guiding Avery College. As evidenced by his view of the importance of supporting women in positions of authority in the Pittsburgh School of Design for Women, and the experience of the Hussey Institute, it is likely that he approved of the succession of Black presidents of Avery College and of a board that was two-thirds Black, but when it came to the crucial test of financial guidance or support, he does not appear to have played an important role. His financial support to institutions was typically for current expenses or one-time capital needs.

Because of its enormous size, Avery's estate distribution was more along the lines of endowment funds. Moreover, the Avery estate was distinct from the college, and while one of the three executors was Hussey's partner Thomas M. Howe, if Hussey advocated for a share for Avery College, there is no evidence of such an effort. Meanwhile, without Avery, the various interpretations of how best to serve African Americans, either free antebellum Blacks or freed post-Civil War Blacks, ultimately destroyed his college.

Avery, like many early abolitionists in the 1820s, was a supporter of African colonization. Colonizationists believed that the best solution to the slavery issue was for African Americans to recolonize Africa, where they could live as free and independent people.[240] There were, however, differing views among whites as to why to support colonization. Some believed the United States to be too corrupted by slavery to ever right the wrong and fully accept Blacks, whereas others thought that Blacks lacked the capacity ever to fully integrate as "true" Americans.

The latter view quickly came to dominate the colonization movement, which was led by the American Colonization Society. During the antebellum period, the A.C.S. allied with many colleges to exclude Blacks. "Rather, advocates of African colonization sought to block avenues of intellectual and social advancement to free Blacks that they thought, ought and should not be permitted to flourish here in America."[241] Such views were not Avery's and he had shifted away from colonization by1834,[242] whereas those with the more racist view of Blacks continued to support colonization. In addition to Howe, the Avery executors included William M. Shinn and Josiah King.

Of the three, Shinn was closest in philosophy to Avery,[243] but he died in 1865 before the estate was distributed. The more conservative executors, Howe and King, were freer to act against Avery's intent and the wishes of Shinn. They distributed the largest part of Avery's estate to the American Missionary Society, whose aim was to spread Christianity in Africa, which was in accordance with Avery's will that half his estate go to that cause.[244] However, this stipulation offered an opening for the conservative estate trustees to support Lincoln University, Avery College's cross-state rival, whose main purpose was training African missionaries.[245]

Colonization was not the only line of cleavage among those supporting Black education. Integration vs. Black-only was itself a conundrum. While Black-only allowed for substantial Black control of the institution, many leading Black abolitionists were opposed to Black-only education. Men like Frederick Douglass characterized it dismissively as "caste" education:

> Whether white scholars are to be admitted or excluded, the circular of the Institute does not inform us. The exclusive principle, if it prevails, will be a great bar to the usefulness of the institution. Now that so many of our Colleges are open to colored students, they will not be likely to resort to an institution whose benefits are proffered to them upon the condition that they shall recognize themselves as belonging to a distinct *caste*."[246]

Douglass and others may have had an overly rosy view of opportunities for Blacks in 19th-century education but were prescient in dismissing the dead end of "separate but equal".

Avery saw his institution as providing a full-fledged academic curriculum in a college led by and controlled by Blacks. But the executors who could have provided adequate funding for that purpose were more interested in supporting colleges that not only were focused on African missionary work, but that were controlled by whites, such as Lincoln University[247], or schools that emphasized practical vocational training over rigorous academic education, such as the Hampton Normal and Agricultural Institute in Virginia.[248] White-controlled Lincoln University got $20,000 and Avery College nothing from the distribution of the Avery estate, while another Black-run college, Wilberforce University in Ohio got half of what Lincoln did, and with strings attached.[249]

AVERY COLLEGE AND CHURCH AT THE CORNER OF NASH AND AVERY STREETS ON THE NORTH SIDE

A 1960s view of the former Avery College[251]

The building erected for Avery College at the corner of Nash and Avery Streets in in 1850 continued as a trade school in often uneasy co-location with the mission church in accordance with the original charter. It was named the Avery Trade School for Colored Youth, but often still referred to as Avery College in contemporary newspapers. The trade school closed in 1914, and the building remained the home of the Avery Memorial African Methodist Episcopal Church until 1969 when it was demolished for the construction of Interstate 279.[250]

While he was leading the Avery College Board, Hussey was active as founding president of the Freedmen's Aid Commission of Western Pennsylvania, Eastern Ohio, and Western Virginia. Founded December 29, 1864, the announcement of this commission asked for "Donations of Clothing, Bedding Boots, and Shoes, School and other Books and Money to be sent to Rev. J.S.. Travelli, Chairman Executive Committee, at C.G. Hussey & Co.'s No. 37 Fifth Street, Pittsburgh." Hussey's frequent collaborators Thomas M. Howe and William Thaw were among the four vice- presidents.[252]

In December 1865 the Pittsburgh commission celebrated its first anniversary, stating that its purpose was "...to give physical success, mental and moral training to the freedmen." Hussey led the massive meeting, which was addressed by William Lloyd Garrison and a variety of other abolitionist and civil rights leaders, all of whom spoke in uncompromising terms of the requirement for complete social and political equality for Blacks, of the unnaturalness of racism, of the danger of continuing slavery in practice if not name, and of the need for massive resources to educate and provide for the capital needs of the newly freed but impoverished populace. At this meeting, the Pittsburgh commission made a point of stating that they were not intending to supersede more local associations with the same aims. Moreover, the corresponding secretary asserted that their:

...design is rather to concentrate the national influence in favor of the elevation of the freed people and use appropriate means to secure favorable legislation in their behalf. It is really an auxiliary to the Freedmen's Bureau and holds constant communication with it through a secretary located in Washington City.

The Freedmen's Bureau was the formal government body founded at the close of the Civil War and led by General O.O. Howard to assist the newly liberated slaves in adapting to free life.

At the December meeting the secretary reported that the commission had raised $16,000 in cash and goods during the first year, most of which went for emergency support for newly freed slaves, but that they hoped to move away from direct physical support to more permanent assistance such as education, proposing to raise $100,000. Major donations announced at the meeting totaled $3500, with Hussey pledging $1000, double that of the next highest donor, Thomas M. Howe.[253]

Pittsburgh Observatory

Original Allegheny Observatory, 1861[254]

In 1859 three Pittsburgh men, Professor Lewis Bradley, Josiah King, and Harvey Childs, met to consider the purchase of a telescope to place on the top of a house. The scope of the project expanded, as did the number of men involved. It was determined to build an observatory. After the combination of a gift of land from a Mr. Ferguson and Washington McClintoch, and the purchase of an additional parcel from a Mr. Ashworth, the group had assembled a plot of ten acres upon which to construct the observatory and raised enough money to buy a thirteen-inch telescope.

The Allegheny Telescope Association incorporated on March 22, 1860, and was formally constituted on May 15. Hussey was elected president. As usual, many of Hussey's industrial associates or competitors were involved: the other Board members were Thomas M. Howe, William Thaw, Josiah King, and John H. Schoenberger. James Park Jr. was elected secretary.[255] By January 1861, the observatory was open.

64

On November 17, 1863, Philotus Dean was appointed director, the same man who had served earlier as the first president of Avery College, before the three successive African American presidents.[256] Just as the same Pittsburgh industrialists – Hussey, Howe, Park, Phipps, Thaw -- gathered in ever-changing combinations in their philanthropic interests, so, too did many of the same academics whose ventures were supported by the industrialists show up in multiple venues over their careers.

While the Allegheny Telescope Association had successfully built, furnished, and staffed the observatory, its finances were not in good order. With a debt of $12,000, the board determined that the best way forward was to pay off the debts, raise an endowment, and convey the observatory to the Western University of Pennsylvania (now University of Pittsburgh). Hussey and others subscribed $15,000 to pay off the debts, leaving $3000 as seed money for a $20,000 endowment. William Thaw contributed the remaining $17,000. The observatory became part of the university on July 1, 1867.

In August, Professor Samuel Pierpont Langley was appointed Director. Langley had a distinguished scientific career at the observatory, contributing 54 papers to scientific journals while Directory, then becoming head of the Smithsonian in 1890.[257] Thaw remained the great benefactor of the Observatory even after the university absorbed it, but Hussey continued to support it as well. In 1881 Thaw contributed most of the money for an extension but Hussey himself provided $500. [258] Both Hussey and Thaw are listed, with Josiah King, as the members of the Observatory Committee of the university after the school absorbed it. [259] The original observatory was replaced by a new one in 1912.

The pride of the Observatory was its 13-inch telescope[260]

Other Colleges

Beyond institutions in which he was a principal, Hussey was also long associated with several other colleges. He was a trustee of the Western University of Pennsylvania (now the University of Pittsburgh) from 1864 until his death in 1893.[261] He also served as a long-time trustee of the Pennsylvania College for Women (founded as the Pittsburgh Female Academy and now Chatham University) serving from 1879 to 1891.[262]

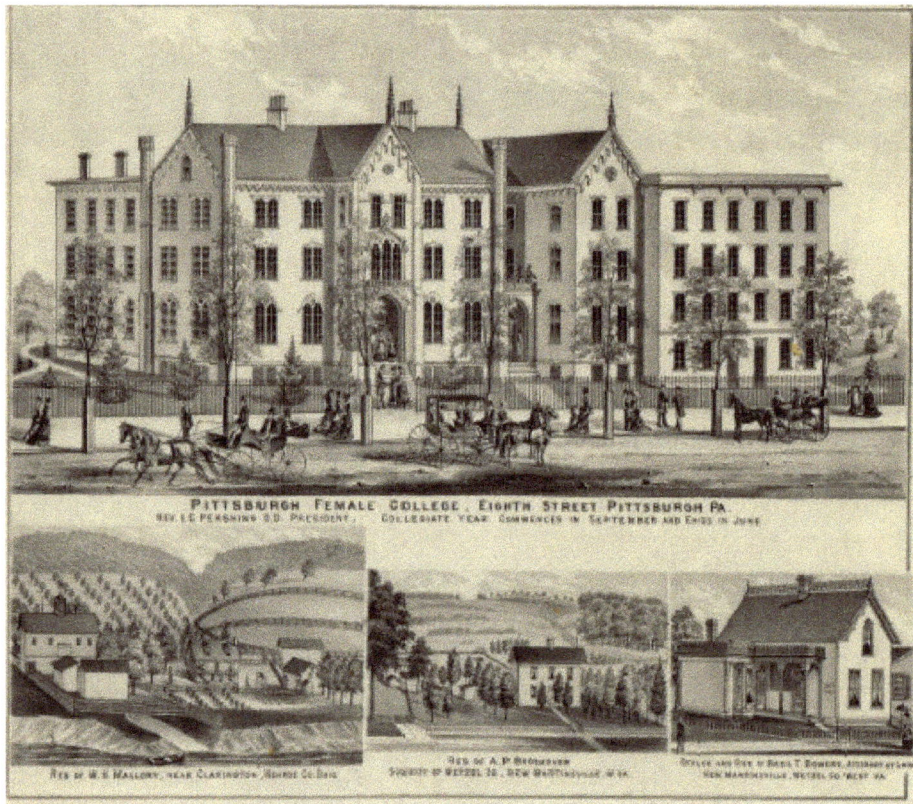

The Pittsburgh Female College, later Pennsylvania College for Women, now Chatham College, in 1877[263]

The Pennsylvania College for Women's original site was on Eighth Street. The current location of Chatham University is, in part, situated on land previously owned by Hussey's long-time associate, Thomas M. Howe.

Hussey was reported to have made contributions to "schools in Tennessee, in North Carolina, in Indian Territory…" and to Earlham College[264], a co-educational Quaker college founded in Earlham, Indiana in 1847. This is consistent with his early years in Indiana, the Quaker affiliation, and the fact that Earlham contributed teachers to the Hussey Institute in Mexico. The North Carolina reference is likely to Guilford College, the other Quaker college that was so intimately connected to the Hussey Institute in Matamoros.

There is little evidence for the extent of Hussey's role in the educational institutions that he supported, even the ones in which he played a major role as a founder,

66

president of a board, or major donor, such as the Pittsburgh School of Design for Women, Avery College, the Pittsburgh Observatory, or the Hussey Institute for Girls. However, the longevity of his tenures and his often-reoccurring financial support speak to a substantial commitment. As in his businesses, he seemed to support institutions on the cutting edge, in these cases of movements such as women's rights, science, or in support of African Americans, often being found at the very inception of these initiatives.

This early-adopter mentality suggests a boldness, even rashness, which is consistent with the chances he took in developing the modern copper and steel industries. But in both spheres, business and philanthropy, there is also specific evidence of his willingness to make quick and profound decisions based on little but a brief meeting with a stranger. In meeting with the ambitious druggist John Hays, Hussey had seen something that gave him the confidence to sponsor Hays' trip to the copper country and then to up the ante substantially when Hays came home with a proposal. Similarly, in the philanthropic vein, he once was visited at home by a Rev. W.K. Brown, who was desperately soliciting to save Cincinnati Wesleyan University from closing. Hussey committed $10,000 but only on condition that Brown and his wife go there and run it. According to a contemporary article in the *Western Christian Advocate*, since it was a women's college, Hussey was insistent that Mrs. Brown play a key role at the school, and she did, becoming a teacher. The article also noted with admiration that Hussey, though a Quaker, was willing to commit so lavishly to a sectarian Methodist school.[265]

Other Charitable Interests

Hussey's specific charitable bequests at his death provide an insight into other charitable interests, some of which were remarked upon during his life.

- The Poor Woman [sic] of Allegheny County were to receive $50,000, dispersed by his executors in equal amounts in Allegheny City and Pittsburgh, apparently not to any particular institution.

- The Peace Association of the Society of Friends of the West, the Hussey School in Matamoros, and the Asylum for Colored Children in Allegheny City each received $5000.

- The Friends Foreign Mission received $1000[266]

Another charity that Hussey supported was the Colored Orphans' Home Founded in 1881 by women of Pittsburgh and Allegheny City, the Colored Orphans' Home in 1896 occupied about two acres on Termon Avenue in Allegheny City and was serving about fifty boys between the age of two and fourteen. Hussey contributed to its construction.[267]

Drawing of Colored Orphans' Home or Asylum for Colored Children in 1896[268]

The Hussey footprint in Pittsburgh

In addition to the sprawling rolling mill at Second Street on the Monongahela River, the steelworks at Penn and 17th and the C.G Hussey & Co. offices and warehouse at 49 Fifth Avenue, Hussey owned two prime residential plots in Allegheny City and Pittsburgh. The Husseys' residence until 1866 was on Cedar Avenue in Allegheny City. When C.G and Rebecca Hussey moved to Shadyside in 1866, their son Christopher Curtis Hussey and his family remained on Cedar Street. Christopher's widow, Harriet, lived there until her death in 1922. The following 1890 map shows the Cedar Street residence, across from East Park (Allegheny Commons), near the 9th Street bridge on the north side of the Allegheny River and almost directly across the river from the steelworks.

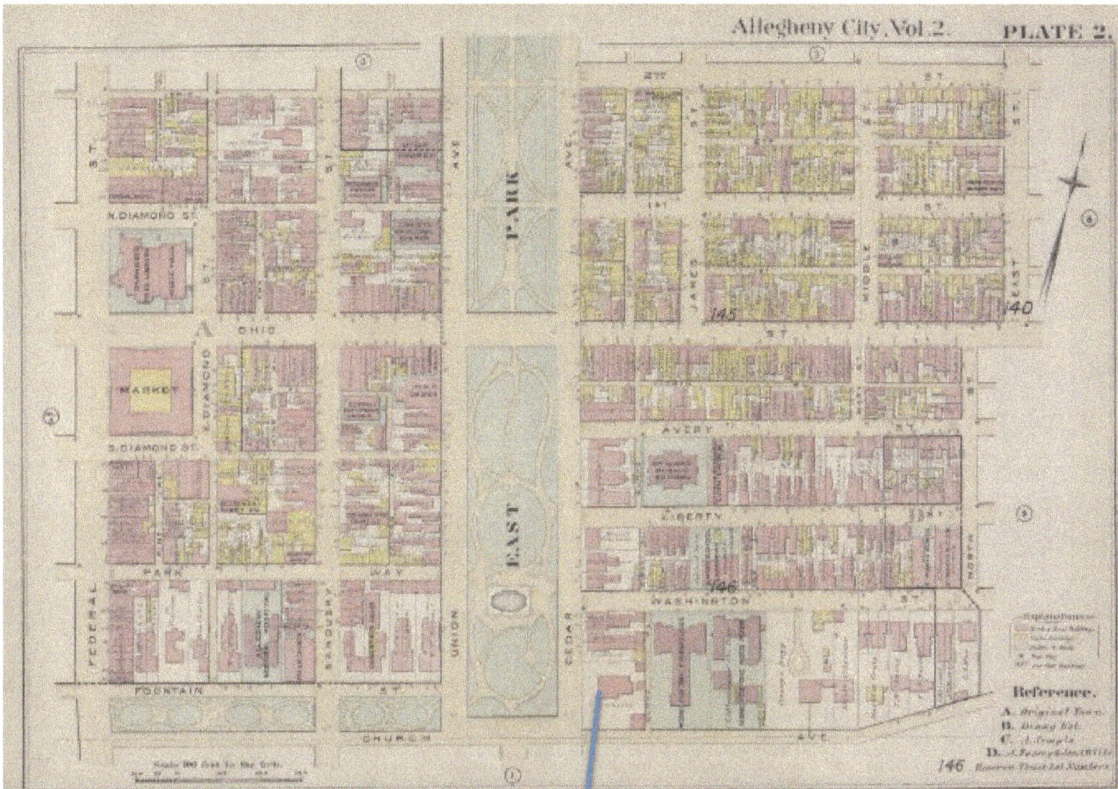

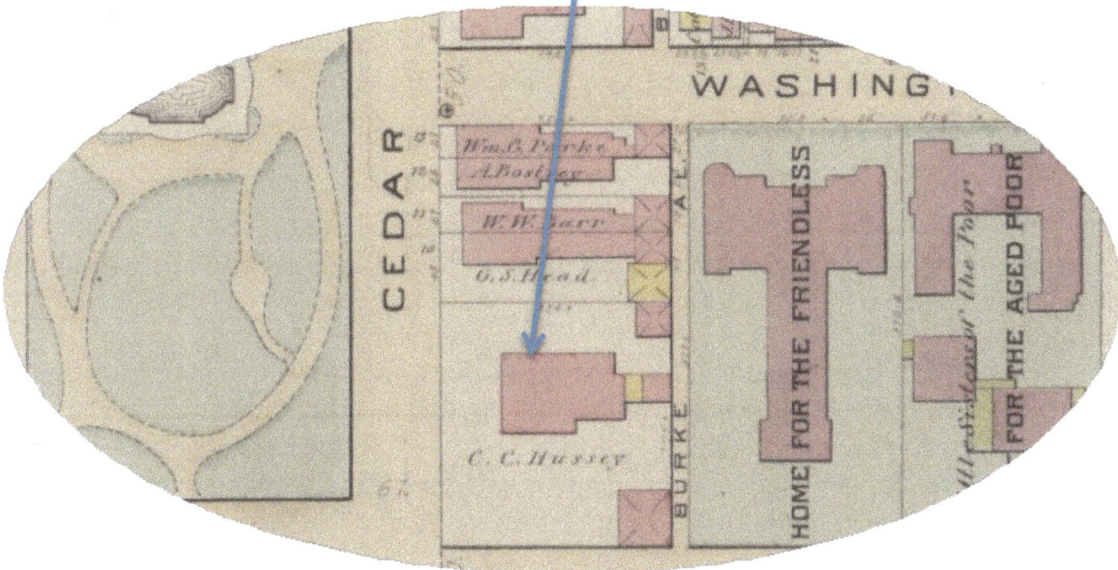

Hussey residence on Cedar Avenue, Allegheny City ,1890[269]

In this map, the house backs up on the Allegheny Home for the Friendless, another institution supported by Hussey,[270] with Allegheny Commons to the left.

In another example of combining civic, philanthropic, and personal interests, C.G. Hussey had been one of the group that founded the Allegheny Commons/East Park across Cedar Ave from his Allegheny City house. A group petitioned the Common Council of the City of Allegheny on August 1, 1857:

> The undersigned, your petitioners, impressed with the belief that the Common grounds, when improved in conformity with some well digested plan, will make Allegheny one of the most pleasant and desirable places of residence in the United States, and enhance in value the real estate within her limits to such extent, as will very materially increase her revenue...[271]

The petitioners asked to be appointed as trustees. The petitioners gave up any claims on the Common ground and asked for the right to raise subscriptions for the construction of the public park, to have control of the planning, and to remain in charge as trustees.

The park was designed by the landscape firm of Mitchell and Grant, opening in 1867. The National Parks Service notes the significance of Allegheny Commons within the context of the mid-19th-century urban park movement. Allegheny Commons became part of Pittsburgh with the 1907 annexation of Allegheny City:

With a period of significance extending from 1868 to 1967, Allegheny Commons is the oldest public park in Pittsburgh, the city's only formal urban park, and one of the first public parks developed west of the Allegheny Mountains.[272]

In typical early-adopter style, C.G. and Rebecca Hussey left Allegheny City and relocated to Shadyside at the onset of its rise to prominence as a newly fashionable section of Pittsburgh's elite. As described in a history of the newly founded Pennsylvania College for Women:

> ..Shadyside in 1860 was a community of about twenty families in an area extending east and west from South Negley to Neville Street and north and south from Centre to Fifth Avenue.[273]

In 1866 the Husseys purchased a tract of between 5 and 6 acres[274] nestled up against the railway curve by the Shadyside railway station (now the Martin Luther King Busway). There they built a mansion that they both lived in for the rest of their lives at 5200 Centre Avenue. The estate occupied about half of the land between the railroad and Aiken Avenue as shown on this 1872 map:

TWENTIETH WARD.

PITTSBURGH.

Scale 600 Feet per Inch.

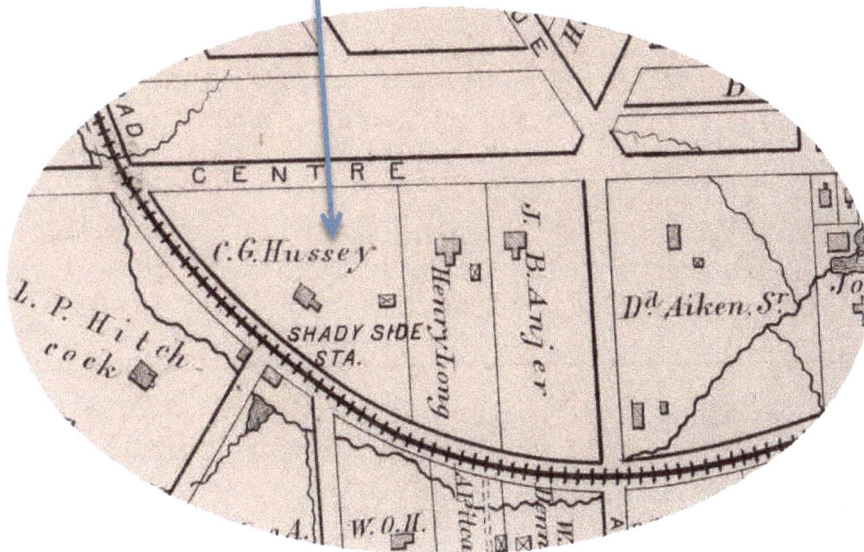

The University of Pittsburgh Medical Center/Shadyside now occupies the land.

Contemporary accounts suggest that both Curtis and Rebecca kept a low social profile. For example, Cushing quotes a "gentleman who has a long, personal, intimate acquaintance" as characterizing Hussey as

..quiet and retiring, and although so widely known through his enterprises, he is seen and known but little in a social way....His very modesty and diffidence sometimes give an impression of austerity which a more intimate acquaintance would remove, for he is affable, considerate, and easily approached...Though a good talker, and having an abundance of valuable information and sound views to impart, he is nevertheless a good listener, and will hear with attention and just appreciation what the humblest individual may have to say.[275]

Numerous contemporary short biographical entries reflect this somewhat hagiographic interpretation of Hussey's character. However, there is enough evidence in specific actions he took in both his business enterprises and his social activism to lend credence to a view of him as being curious as well as far-sighted, willing to hear and act upon novel suggestions quite quickly and being unafraid to put trust in much younger and less established people.

Whether or not his apparently retiring nature was due to natural modesty, his Quaker beliefs, or both, C.G Hussey's private life remains primarily a mystery. Rebecca is even more obscure, as would be expected from the wife of an industrialist who herself was a pious and retiring Quaker and who did not socialize much. A rare contemporary account in 1888 presents a similarly approving view of her:

Mrs. C. G. Hussey, wife of Dr. Hussey, the great steel manufacturer, whose wealth is computed at from ten to twelve millions, is as far removed from fashionable life, through choice, as though she were obliged to abstain for want of sufficient means. In disposition she is singularly modest and retiring. Her mind is of the highest order intellectually, and she possesses the delightful accomplishment of reading aloud remarkably well. Mrs. Hussey is enthusiastic in the temperance movement. They live in an immense house at Shadyside, which is filled with bronzes and fine statuary. Their conservatory is one of the finest in the city.[276]

Yet, what little evidence there is of her public life revolves around causes. In 1875 Rebecca Hussey made a grand gesture by escorting a former slave, reputed to be 112 years old, to a tea party, as related in an unsourced newspaper article:

Veritable Centenarian.

Colored Man 112 Years Old - One Who really Knows His Age.

At the Tea Party Matinee, Saturday afternoon, there was present a veritable centenarian - a colored man who had reached the age of 112 years. He was escorted by Mrs. C.G. Hussey, and attracted no small share of attention.

The old man was agile to a remarkable degree for one of his age. His name is Frank Wentt. He was born on Col. Isaac Zane's plantation, sixteen miles from Winchester, in Shenandoah county, Va., January 16, 1763. After he grew up he was sold to Col. David Lupton, who had a plantation four miles west of Winchester. The Colonel gave Frank, who was then a slave, to his daughter Ann, who afterward married Nathan Updegraff, Mrs. Hussey's grandfather, through whose family he descended down to Dr. Hussey, whose ward the old man is at present.

Frank has lived to see Gen. George Washington and nearly all the great men since that time, and had the pleasure of seeing his race freed from the thraldom of slavery. Beside him on the stage where he sat on Saturday stood a descendant in the sixth generation of his former master, Updegraff, in a little son of Mr. C.C. Hussey. Uncle Frank has a wife ninety-four years old, and he is furnished a house in the city during the winter by his kind benefactor, and one in the country (at Sewickley) in summer. The old man said In regard to his country home: "I've soon gwine out dar." In answer to a question whether he remembered anything of former years the old *man said:...(The rest of the article is missing.)*[277]

Rebecca is also listed as a signatory of the Declaration of Rights Of the Women of the United States by the National Woman 1881, written by the abolitionist and women's rights activist Matilda Joslyn Gage.[278]

For all their economic success, the Husseys endured a continuous string of family tragedies throughout out their married life. They had five children, born between 1840 and 1852, only one of whom outlived Curtis and Rebecca. Their fourth child, James, died aged 4. Daughters Mary Hussey Guthrie and Anna Hussey Binns died at 22 and 27, respectively. Their first-born, Christopher Curtis Hussey died of a stroke at age 43 in 1884[279], leaving only Emma Hussey Alsop as the surviving child. She outlived her parents but died in 1907 at the age of 55.

Christopher's premature death was particularly notable since he had been active in Hussey's businesses from a very early age. He was also a partner with his brother-in-law and cousin, Edward Binns, in Hussey & Binns, founded in 1874, likely with assistance from C.G. Hussey. Binns died in 1877 at the age of 36, only six years after the death of his wife Anna. Edward Binns died in San Francisco, where he had reportedly gone for his health.[280] The orphaned young children of Anna Hussey and Edward Binns, Edward Hussey Binns and Ralph Holden Binns (born in 1866 and 1869, respectively), joined their grandparents at Shadyside and went on to be active in the various businesses. C.G. and Rebecca's daughter Emma also lived with the Husseys at Shadyside even after her marriage to Edward Alsop, remaining there until her death in 1907.

Christopher Hussey's sudden death on a trip to Florida in 1884 elicited this letter to C.G. Hussey from James Adair, whom Hussey had hired in 1859 as a financial manager for the new steelworks:

DEAR SIR:-There are times when grief is so sacred, and the stricken household such holy ground, that even the voice of Sympathy should he hushed, its footfalls unheard, and its tears unseen, and when all it would say or do should be entrusted to the silent messenger who asks no audience, wearies no time, nor taxes the heavy laden for an answering word. Through him I send all my sympathy. Words of comfort, philosophy and religion are vain, for the hours of suffering have come. Nevertheless, God and his great high priest, Time, ever live and reign, and as the days softly step upon the troubled mind, they say, "peace, he still," and lo, in a little while a great calm shall come.

I shall miss Curtis a great deal, for we have worked together for over a score of years, beginning with our young manhood. If " labor is worship," in all religion he set us an example. Industry and duty praise him, while gentleness, kindness and charity, which is forgiveness, claim him as their boy. And if I miss him, how can I estimate your loss without the infinite factor of a father's love for an only son, with which to make the multiplication. God knows the answer, but he will soon begin to rub away the long line of figures with his own kind hand.

Yours with great respect and regard,
James Adair[281]

With Christopher Hussey's death, the only alternative to passing down the businesses was through his grandsons. Although in 1888 he gave up the Hussey interest in the steel company he had founded, he maintained the copper company. The Hussey-Binns Shovel company that had been led by Christopher Hussey and Edward Binns continued in business, both of these businesses passing to the grandsons when they were old enough to manage them.

Personal Wealth

Prosperous as was from his pork trading business, Hussey was propelled into the ranks of the very wealthy in the 1840s through the success of the copper juggernaut, including the Cliff mine, the Pittsburgh Copper and Brass Rolling Mills and the C.G. Hussey & Co, and then through the Hussey, Wells & Co. steel enterprise, starting ins 1859. He is estimated to have been Pittsburgh's richest man by the 1860s:

Pittsburgh's four principal crucible steelmakers were the Hussey, Wells partnership, whose success made Curtis Hussey into the city's first millionaire; Black Diamond Steel, run by native Pittsburghers James and David Park; the Sheffield Steelworks, owned by a prominent Pittsburgh partnership; and Crescent Steel, owned by Pittsburghers and run by a native Englishman. By 1877, the region's fourteen medium-scale crucible steel factories produced nearly three-fourths of the nation's output.[282]

If the R.G Dun report of 1851 is accurate, he was probably already a millionaire based just on his pork business, let alone the copper wealth, well before he made money in steel. During the Civil War, the income of those paying the 5% federal income tax was published in the newspapers. A suggestion of Hussey's wealth in the 1860s is suggested by his reported 1866 income of about $100,000 (roughly $1.5 million in 2017), second only to William Thaw's $157,000 in Allegheny County.[283] Carnegie at this time was still catching up at $42,000 in 1863 and $56,000 in 1867, enough to be considered a millionaire by contemporaries, but not in the front ranks like Thaw or Hussey.[284]

While the R.G Dun reports, the few extant corporate reports, and scattered contemporary newspaper accounts suggest both prudence and more wealth than can be neatly quantified, a common theme in the short contemporary biographies of the time typically note Hussey's high reputation as a conservative manager of money. For example, from this 1889 biography of the aged steel man:

> Dr. Hussey's business practices since coming to Pittsburgh have been somewhat unusual in one respect, which is that in his mining and manufacturing enterprises, and in investments in property, he has never borrowed any money, and it has been his custom to keep large reserves of cash in his different concerns.[285]

The sources of Hussey's personal wealth are varied but evident. What is not clear is a definitive figure for that wealth at his death or in the years leading up to death. A likely estimate is at least $10 million. The 1889 estimate of his wealth at over $1 million early in the days of Hussey, Wells & Co., was followed by additional estimates in his later years. In 1885, a report that was widely circulated among American newspapers estimated his worth at $6 million, the same as his friend William Thaw, and behind only four other Pittsburgh estates. Wealthiest was Mary Schenley, estimated at $25 million followed by Andrew Carnegie at $15 million, which gives context to the enormous fortunes of those listed. There were thirty-one Pittsburgh residents estimated to be worth at least $1 million and the article's subtitle touts "More rich men in proportion to population than any city in the union".[286] Hussey's obituary in the *Pittsburgh Post Gazette* estimated his wealth at $10 million[287] and the *Pittsburgh Dispatch* offered the wider range of $10-$20 million[288] and *The Social Mirror* estimated $10-12 million in 1888.[289]

Hussey died on April 25, 1893, at the age of 90, from a broken neck suffered in a fall. His will, written in 1889, made specific bequests totaling just over $1.1 million in cash and bonds, and divided any remainder in 1/7s for seven grandchildren. In addition, he bequeathed the estate at Shadyside to his wife Rebecca and all the real and financial assets of the Pittsburgh Copper and Brass Rolling Mills and the C.G. Hussey & Co. to his grandsons Edward Hussey Binns, Ralph Holden Binns, and Curtis Grubb Hussey, the son Christopher Hussey. Other real estate included various houses in Pittsburgh and a warehouse in Philadelphia at 523 Market Street, now part of land of the national monument that includes Independence Hall.[290]

The total probate inventory at the Allegheny County Orphans Court dated June 20, 1893 is valued at $2,583,300.08.[291] This suggests that all the real estate listed in the will, as well as the highly prosperous rolling mill and C.G. Hussey & Co itself had a total value of only $1.6 million, and that any proceeds from his 1888 sale of his share of the vast

Hussey, Howe & Co steelworks was included in the $1.1 million in cash and bonds. According to multiple limited partnership agreements from the 1880s among the Hussey, Howe & Co. owners, "The aggregate capital of such association shall be One Million Dollars". Of that, $496,000 was apportioned to Mary Ann Howe, Thomas Howe's widow, $333,000 to C.G. Hussey, $167,000 to C.C. Hussey, and $4,000 to James Brown.[292]

The estate value at death does not seem to accurately reflect the assets listed in the will, such as his real estate, including the estate at Shadyside, but also does not seem to reflect other assets referred to in various places. The Boston Globe obituary was titled "Dr. C.G. Hussey is Dead – Was Richest Man in Pittsburg and an American Copper King. The subtitle "Was Richest Man in Pittsburg" seems an overstatement by 1893, but refers to a series of assets not apparent from this will: "He was one of the leading stockholders of the *Chronicle-Telegraph*, the second oldest afternoon newspaper here… He was the heaviest owner of real estate in the central portion of Pittsburg and constantly had $4,000,000 to $5,000,000 loaned out on mortgage."[293]

However, the essay also erroneously says that he was "a member of the shovel manufacturing firm of Hussey, Binns & Co." Although he may have staked his son and son-in-law in founding this company, he was not directly involved.

In another isolated measurement of his assets, the C.G. Hussey & Co. headquarters building on Fifth Avenue alone was assessed by the city in 1892 at $641,600, over his protests.[294] This building was part of the copper business inherited by the three grandsons and probably was considered part of that operation. There remain scattered hints at yet additional parts of the estate not mentioned in the will or elsewhere.

One group of assets not accounted for in the will included remaining interests in the Michigan copper lands. The Cliff Mine had been sold in 1871, but Hussey and his partners retained ownership of other tracts, which had been bought early on in anticipation of replicating the success of the Cliff. These lands came to be called the Hussey-Howe-Cooper lands and were owned not corporately, but individually by the heirs to C.G. Hussey, Thomas M. Howe, James Cooper, and to descendants of the minority Boston partners in Hussey's mining ventures.

In 1907, Edward Grew of the Isle Royal mining company, which surrounded one tract on three sides, made an offer. Even in 1907 a tangle of heirs was almost impossible to unravel in order to effect a sale. James W. Brown and Edward Hussey Binns successfully led an effort to answer the appeal and sold the 280 acre chunk for $225,000. The Hussey estate share came to $55,000.[295] This sale turned out to be a wise move, a last chance for profit on the fading mineral fortunes of the Keweenaw Peninsula that had made C.G Hussey a very rich man. The remaining Hussey-Howe- Cooper lands in the area were reorganized into a Declaration of Trust to the Superior Trust Company in 1916[296] and languished for over 70 years until sold in 1979. The Hussey share from the final liquidation of the eight remaining Hussey- Howe-Cooper tracts was just under $30,000 in 1979 dollars, divided among dozens of C.G. Hussey heirs.[297] These examples do not exhaust the possibilities of assets not accounted for in Hussey's will, but they do raise questions as to the true extent of his assets at death.

An estate value of about $2.7 million does not seem to come close to contemporary estimates of his wealth or that of his peers at the time, nor of a man who as early as the 1850s was considered a millionaire and the richest man in Pittsburgh. The estimate of at least $10 million is not only plausible, but also likely, and conservative. An estate of $10-$20 million in1893 translates into a minimum of $250-$500 million in 2017. Even the lesser figure of $2.7 million would minimally be $67.5 million in 2017.

Glossary

Many of the technical terms related to copper and steel are arcane. They may not be critical to understanding the story of Curtis Grubb Hussey, but definitions might be useful to the curious reader.

amygdaloid	Igneous rock with pure metal in amygdules, almond shaped cavities
azurite	See Marlachite
billet	A length of steel with a rectangular or round cross section of smaller dimension than a bloom, formed from a bloom or ingot (see also ingot, bloom)
black copper oxide, black copper, copper oxide, or melaconite	Oxides and carbonites which appear close to surface where air and water can react with the metal
blister steel	An alloy of iron and carbon produced by the cementation process, and a flux to help remove impurities (see cementation)
cast iron	A group of iron-carbon alloys with a carbon content greater than 2%. (2-4% carbon), but also other alloys manganese and silicon as well as impurities such as sulfur and phosphorous. Cast iron is brittle, comparatively hard and non-malleable compared to wrought iron. It fractures before bending but has good compression strength and was used in building before steel.
cementation	Process of heating layers of iron bars and carbon for 6-8 days, constantly checking (see also blister steel)
conglomerate	Puddingstone; pebbles cemented together with pure copper metal
copper mineral	Product of a stamp mill (or a concentrate) before shipment to the smelter for final elimination of nonmetallic materials

copper rock	Tiny pieces of highly disseminated metal embedded in a rock matrix, which has not yet been sent to the stamp mill for crushing and elimination of waste
cupola furnace	Top of a reverberatory furnace, for treating slags that are the waste byproduct of copper smelting
crucible steel	Steel produced in clay crucible pots and poured out into ingots to cool
direct process	Crucible steel produced directly from pig iron rather than from blister steel
float copper	Surface copper
flux	Any substance introduced in the smelting of ores to promote fluidity and remove impurities – typically limestone
Ingot	The rough form of the metal when first cooled and congealed, shaped by the mold into which it was poured after smelting (See also bloom, billet)
Kibble	Buckets for hauling out ore, holding up to 1 ton
Marlachite	Green carbonite of copper, also know as azurite
mass copper/copper mass	Solid piece of native or pure copper weighing 100 pounds or more and embedded in a rock matrix.
overflow deposits	Copper that cooled and congealed on or near the surface
pig iron	Intermediate product of smelting iron ore. It is the molten iron from the blast furnace, which is a large and cylinder-shaped furnace charged with iron ore, coke, and limestone. Charcoal and anthracite have also been used as fuel. Pig iron is brittle but refined product (often cast in ingots) which was usually sold to other companies and turned into wrought iron or steel
puddling	The process of creating wrought iron or steel from the pig iron produced in a blast furnace. The furnace is constructed to pull the hot air over the iron without the

fuel coming into direct contact with the iron, a system generally known as a reverberatory furnace or open hearth furnace. The major advantage of this system is keeping the impurities of the fuel separated from the charge.

open hearth A modification of puddling, dramatically increasing the temperatures to which the pig iron was subjected and so removing carbon without requiring the efforts of a puddler. "regenerative principle" - Siemens used the waste gases to generate yet more heat.

stamping The process of separating small pieces of copper from rock and other impurities. Stamping consists of a set of heavy steel (iron-shod wood in some cases) stamps, loosely held vertically in a frame, in which the stamps can slide up and down. They are lifted by cams on a horizontal rotating shaft. As the cam moves from under the stamp, the stamp falls onto the ore below, crushing the rock, and the lifting process is repeated at the next pass of the cam.

teeming Pouring of the molten steel from the crucible, which be must be done slowly and steadily and directly to the bottom of the receiving mold.

types of steel production Bessemer, crucible, open hearth, puddled, cementation, blister (see specific types)

wheels warf Grit from grinding stones, used to cover iron/charcoal in chests that produce steel by cementation. Grit contains mix of rion, steel, and their oxides in small portions mixed with the grit, which fuses to a cindery slag keeping steel from action of air.

wrought iron

An iron alloy with a very low carbon (less than 0.08%) content in contrast to cast iron (2% to 4%). It is primarily iron, with small amounts,1-2%,slag of silicon, sulfer, phosphorous, aluminum oxides. Wrought iron is softer and more ductile than cast iron and can be reheated and reworked into other shapes. It has higher tensile strength, is resistant to fatigue, and was used in horizontal construction bars before steel

Other Hussey Enterprises

The Cliff Mine was the bonanza that seeded Hussey's rise from prosperity to great wealth and Hussey, Wells & Co steel redoubled that wealth. However, Hussey invested in many other mining ventures, none of which provided remotely as valuable as the Cliff. He also was a founder or officer in many bank and insurance companies.

Following is a list of mines in which Hussey, Thomas Howe, or Charles Avery, the main investors in the Cliff, was an officer, and in all of which Hussey was likely an investor, as well as some of the other businesses in which he played a role.

Mine	Location	Date	Notes
Adventure Mining Co.	Likely MI	1846	
Husse Mining Co.	Likely MI	1850	
Central Mining Co	Michigan	1854	
Copper Harbor Mining Co.	Michigan		
Dacotah Mining Co 1			
Great Western Mining Co.			
Hussey & Howe Mining Co.	New York		
Mann Mining Co.			
Mass Mining Co.			
Miscowaubik Mining Co.			
National Mining Co.	Colorado	1864	
National Mining Co	Michigan	1854	
North American Mining Co.	Michigan		
North Cliff Mining Co.	Michigan		
North Western Mining Co.			
Swamscott Mining Co			

A silver mining claim	Colorado	1872	

Most of these mines had mediocre results at best, only Central and National (Michigan) being successful.[298] National (Michigan), for example, had in its first three years a net profit of $92,000[299]

The following table contains a partial list of companies in which Hussey was an owner, officer, or director, in addition to his copper and steel interests:

Company	Location	Date	Notes
Hussey, Goss & Co.	Indiana		Pork
Hussey & Wells Pork Packers	Pittsburgh	1855	Or earlier
Hussey, Hays & Co.	Pittsburgh	1850	Pork
Hanna, Hussey & Co	Pittsburgh	1846	Banking, later Hanna, Hart & Co, then Hart, Caughy & Co., first agent for Civil War bonds in Pittsburgh
Real Estate Savings Bank	Pittsburgh	1862	
Allegheny Insurance	Pittsburgh	1854	Possibly earlier
Cumberland Oil Co.	Kentucky	1865	
Hussey Oil Co.	Kentucky	1866	
N.W. Hussey & Co.	Ohio	1864	Woolens
Chronicle-Telegraph			Newspaper

Endnotes

Endnotes for Foreword

[1] *C.G. Hussey*, 1860. Signed C.G. Hussey. Galaxy Pub. Co.
[2] Andrew Carnegie, "The Autobiography of Andrew Carnegie." p. 41.

Endnotes for Tryouts

[3] *A Genealogical and Biographical History of Allegheny County, Pennsylvania*, ed. Thomas Cushing (Baltimore, MD: Genealogical Publishing Co., 2007). p 254.
[4] Daniel J. Ryan, *History of Ohio: The Rise and Progress of an American State*, vol. 4 (New York1912). p. 124.
[5] Phillip R. Shriver and Jr. Wunderlin, Clarence E, *The Documentary Heritage of Ohio* (Athens, Ohio: Ohio University Press, 2000). p. 208.
[6] "Village of Mt. Pleasant," National Park Service, https://www.nps.gov/nr/travel/underground/oh4.htm.
[7] "Notes for Jonathan Binns.", The Pennocks of Primitive Hall, http://www.pennock.ws/surnames/nti/nti11407.html
[8] "Morgan County, Indiana," Wikipedia, https://en.wikipedia.org/wiki/Morgan_County,_Indiana.
[9]*Counties of Morgan, Monroe and Brown, Indiana: Historical and Biographical*, (Chicago: F.A. Battery & Co., 1884). pp. 99, 103.
[10] Ibid. p. 126.
[11] Terry S. Reynolds, "Curtis Grubb Hussey, Smelting/Refining Industry Leaders, Copper Industry Leaders, Meatpackers," (American National Biography Online).
[12] " Indiana Yearly Meeting Minutes, 1823-1833." p. 76.
[13] Ibid. p. 121.

[14] Ibid. p. 127-128.
[15] Ibid. p. 131.
[16] A. H. Hussey, in *Hussey Archives* (Mt. Pleasant Historical Society, 1865).
[17] "Curtis Grubbs Hussey," http://legdb.iga.in.gov/#!/legislator/2172/Curtis-Hussey.
[18] "R.G. Dun Credit Report Volumes 1840-95." 1.193

Endnotes for Copper

[19] Donald Chaput, *The Cliff; America's First Great Copper Mine* (Kalamazoo, Michigan: Sequoia Press, 1971). p. 17. Chaput cites a letter of agreement between Hussey and Hays as being in the Carnegie Public Library, but that document can no longer be found.

[20] Angus Murdoch, *Boom Copper the Story of the First U.S. Mining Boom* (New York: The MacMillan Company, 1945). p. 50. In *Copper Boom*, his witty, comprehensive, but lightly sourced history of this era, Murdock makes this assertion but offers no proof of Hussey's advice to Hays.

[21] Ralph D. Williams, *The Honorable Peter White* (Cleveland Ohio: The Penton Publishing Co., 1907). p. 10.

[22] "Great Lakes Area Map," (Google Maps).

[23] Chaput, *The Cliff; America's First Great Copper Mine.* p. 17.

[24] Williams, *The Honorable Peter White.* p. 113.

[25] William B. Jr. Gates, *Michigan Copper and Boston Dollars an Economic History of the Michigan Copper Mining Industry* (Cambridge, MA: Harvard University Press, 1951). p. 2.

[26] Ibid.

[27] Chaput, *The Cliff; America's First Great Copper Mine.* p. 15.

[28] Donald V. Purn, "Great Copper Rush in Upper Michigan 1842," http://www.oldalgonquin.net/Schooner/copperrush.html.

[29] Chaput, *The Cliff; America's First Great Copper Mine.* pp. 15-16.

[30] Ibid. pp. 11-13.

[31] Charles K. Hyde, *Copper for America: The United States Copper Industry from Colonial Times to the 1990s* (Tuscon: University of Arizona Press, 1998). pp. 7-8. [32] Gates, *Michigan Copper and Boston Dollars an Economic History of the Michigan Copper Mining Industry.* pp. 9-10.

[33] Robert B. Pettengill, "The United States Foreign Trade in Copper 1790-1932," *American Economic Review* XXV (1935). pp 426-427.

[34] Gates, *Michigan Copper and Boston Dollars an Economic History of the Michigan Copper Mining Industry.* pp. 9-10.

[35] Pettengill, "The United States Foreign Trade in Copper 1790-1932." p. 427.

[36] Gates, *Michigan Copper and Boston Dollars an Economic History of the Michigan Copper Mining Industry.* p. 203.

[37] Murdoch, *Boom Copper the Story of the First U.S. Mining Boom.* p. 54.

[38] Chaput, *The Cliff; America's First Great Copper Mine.* p.18. The Magazine of Western History biography of Hussey gives a slightly different accounting of the 1843 ownership, with Hussey, Avery, and Petit holding 1/6 each (4/24), Avery 1/8 (3/24), and Hays with a 1/24 share, for a total of 2/3 held by the Pittsburgh interests, and the remaining 1/3 (8/24) being held by the Boston interests, listed as Talmadge and Raymond in this accounting. p. 334.

[39] *History of the Upper Peninsula of Michigan: Containing a Full Account of Its Early Settlement, Its Growth, Development, and Resources, an Extended Description of Its Iron and Copper Mines,* (Chicago: Western Historical Co., A.T. Andreas Proprietor, 1883).

[40] *The Cliff; America's First Great Copper Mine.* p 34, citing Acts of Legislature 1848, No. 45

[41] Ibid. p. 18.

[42] Ibid. p. 19.

[43] Ibid. p. 22. Murdock (p. 53) offers the figure of $25,000 in expenses.

[44] Murdoch, *Boom Copper the Story of the First U.S. Mining Boom.* P. 49.

[45] Chaput, *The Cliff; America's First Great Copper Mine.* p. 23.

[46] Ibid. p. 19. Referring the 1869 annual report as printed in the *Portage Lake Mining Gazette,* June 16, 1870. This would be one last retrospective boast, as the Cliff Mine was played out and sold that year.

[47] Ibid. p. 22.

[48] Ibid. p. 23.

[49] Murdoch, *Boom Copper the Story of the First U.S. Mining Boom.* p. 54.

[50] Chaput, *The Cliff; America's First Great Copper Mine.* p. 25.

[51] Murdoch, *Boom Copper the Story of the First U.S. Mining Boom.* p. 54. It may not have been Jennings who provided this crucial estimate. According to Chaput, Hussey called in geologist Alfred Rudolf who gave the figure of 800 feet. In any case, the investors called on expert technical advice and acted on it. Similarly, Murdoch and Chaput offer differing amounts that Avery put up on the basis of this advice ($60,000 vs. $80,000) but both agree that he rolled the dice with virtually all the cash he had left. Chaput, *The Cliff; America's First Great Copper Mine.* p.25.

[52] Chaput, *The Cliff; America's First Great Copper Mine.* pp. 33-34.

[53] Murdoch, *Boom Copper the Story of the First U.S. Mining Boom.* p. 56.

[54] Chaput, *The Cliff; America's First Great Copper Mine.* p. 36.

[55] Gates, *Michigan Copper and Boston Dollars an Economic History of the Michigan Copper Mining Industry.* p. 197.

[56] Chaput, *The Cliff; America's First Great Copper Mine.*, citing a report in the *Portage Lake Mining Gazette,* April 13, 1876

[57] George H. Thurston, *Pittsburgh as It Is; or Facts and Figures Exhibiting the Past and Present of Pittsburgh, Its Advantages, Resources, Manufactures, and Commerce* (Pittsburgh: W.S. Haven, 1857). p. 134.

[58] Chaput, *The Cliff; America's First Great Copper Mine.* p. 54.

[59] Gates, *Michigan Copper and Boston Dollars an Economic History of the Michigan Copper Mining Industry.* p. 216.

[60] Thurston, *Pittsburgh as It Is; or Facts and Figures Exhibiting the Past and Present of Pittsburgh, Its Advantages, Resources, Manufactures, and Commerce.* p. 133.

[61] Chaput, *The Cliff; America's First Great Copper Mine.* p. 37, citing Foster and Whitney *Copper Lands*, Plate VIII, Michigan Tech Archives.

[62] Ibid. p. 37, citing Foster and Whitney *Copper Lands*, Plate IX, Michigan Tech Archives.

[63] Ibid. p. 35, citing Foster and Whitney *Copper Lands*, Plate III, Michigan Tech Archives.

[64] Ibid. pp. 32-34.

[65] Gates, *Michigan Copper and Boston Dollars an Economic History of the Michigan Copper Mining Industry.* p. 25.

[66] Ibid. p. 24.

[67] Chaput, *The Cliff; America's First Great Copper Mine.* p. 51, citing Roy Drier, *Copper Country Tales*

[68] Gates, *Michigan Copper and Boston Dollars an Economic History of the Michigan Copper Mining Industry.* p. 37., citing *Portage Lake Mining Gazette,* February 4, 1865.

[69] Ibid. p. 36.

[70] William J Tenney, ed., *Mining Magazine*1855. pp. 88. Gates also describes this lag and the fact that the Cliff Mine was the first to adopt cash-and-carry (p. 36), citing in

footnote 136 (p. 240) the company report for 1853.

[71] Gates, *Michigan Copper and Boston Dollars an Economic History of the Michigan Copper Mining Industry*. p. 28.

[72] (Williams 1907, 139)

[73] "Ship Canal at Sault St. Marie," *Pittsburgh Daily Post*, January 8 1852. p. 3.

[74] Williams, *The Honorable Peter White*. p. 133. Williams notes (p. 136) that the third shipment of ore was by the General Taylor, owned by Hussey & St. Clair of Cleveland. Hussey is likely Joseph Hussey, C. G. Hussey's brother, owner of the copper smelting operation in Cleveland.

[75] "Soo Locks," https://en.wikipedia.org/wiki/Soo_Locks.

[76] Gates, *Michigan Copper and Boston Dollars an Economic History of the Michigan Copper Mining Industry*. p. 10, footnote 32, p.236.

[77] *A Genealogical and Biographical History of Allegheny County, Pennsylvania*. p. 257, Chaput, *The Cliff; America's First Great Copper Mine*. p.58, citing Michigan State Archives. Gates, *Michigan Copper and Boston Dollars an Economic History of the Michigan Copper Mining Industry*. p. 7, footnote 129.

[78] Gates, *Michigan Copper and Boston Dollars an Economic History of the Michigan Copper Mining Industry*. p. 37.

[79] William W. Williams, ed, "Curtis G. Hussey," *Magazine of Western History*1886. p. 340.

[80] Gates, *Michigan Copper and Boston Dollars an Economic History of the Michigan Copper Mining Industry*. p. 8.

[81] Ibid.

[82] Chaput, *The Cliff; America's First Great Copper Mine*. pp. 37-38.

[83] James B. Cooper, "Historical Sketch of Smelting and Refining Lake Copper," *Proceedings of the Lake Superior Mining Institute*, March 5-9 1901. pp. 23-24.

[84] Hyde, *Copper for America: The United States Copper Industry from Colonial Times to the 1990s*. p. 22.

[85] Cooper, "Historical Sketch of Smelting and Refining Lake Copper." pp. 23-24.

[86] Gates, *Michigan Copper and Boston Dollars an Economic History of the Michigan Copper Mining Industry*. p. 20.

[87] Ibid. p. 7.

[88] Thomas Egleston, "Copper Refining in the United States," *Transactions of the American Institute of Mining Engineers May, 1880 to September, 1881*1881. pp. 678- 679, Cooper, "Historical Sketch of Smelting and Refining Lake Copper." p. 23. Eggleston does not state that the Baltimore or Fort Pitt attempts at smelting Lake Superior copper used Cliff Mine copper, but as the Cliff was the first to produce this type of copper in the area, it is likely that copper from 1847 and 1848 was Hussey copper. Egleston's first direct connection of Hussey copper and a smelting attempt was with the Revere works at Point Shirley. Cooper, however, does specify that the Fort Pitt trial was Hussey's.

[89] Egleston, "Copper Refining in the United States." p. 679.

[90] Ibid. p. 680, Cooper, "Historical Sketch of Smelting and Refining Lake Copper." pp. 23-24.

[91] Hyde, *Copper for America: The United States Copper Industry from Colonial Times to the 1990s*. p. 22.

[92] "History," http://www.husseycopper.com/about/history/. In an interesting twist that might please its founder, Hussey Copper is owned by Patriarch Patriarch frPartners LLC, whose founder and CEO (2017) is a woman, Lynn Tilton.

[93] G.M. Hopkins & Co., "Parts of Wards 13 & 14 Pittsburgh Plate 2," (Philadelphia: G.M. Hopkins, 1882).

[94] Hyde, *Copper for America: The United States Copper Industry from Colonial Times to the 1990s.* p. 182.

[95] Egleston, "Copper Refining in the United States." p. 678.

[96] Ibid. p. 681

[97] Ibid. p. 680.

[98] Chaput, *The Cliff; America's First Great Copper Mine.* p. 79. In footnote 21, Chaput recounts his own experience using the same technology worker as a smelter in the 1950s.

[99] Egleston, "Copper Refining in the United States." p. 680-681.

[100] Gates, *Michigan Copper and Boston Dollars an Economic History of the Michigan Copper Mining Industry.* p. 29., Egleston, "Copper Refining in the United States." pp. 679-681. Egleston also notes that a Baltimore copper works had unsuccessfully tried to use a reverberatory furnace to smelt copper in 1847, so Hussey may have been aware of a precedent closer to home than Europe.

[101] Microsoft Bing images "Reverberatory Furnaces": https://www.bing.com/images/search?view=detailV2&ccid=VQHzUmtW&id=4E532883 E68F8DC3CD0F2E989B02F8390DD9A400&thid=OIP.VQHzUmtWiU1RReMximm6bAHaF D&mediaurl=http%3A%2F%2Fwww.coppercountryexplorer.com%2F wp-content%2Fuploads%2Fquincysmelter%2Fanatomy%2Freverb6.jpg&exph=382&e xpw=560&q=image+of+a+reverberatory+furnace&simid=607992475705478609&a jaxhist=0&selectedindex=25

[102] According to Hyde (p. 24) Hussey had employed two Welsh smelters, William and Henry Johns, and Henry Johns' son claimed his father was responsible. Murdoch (p. 56) and Williams (p. 17) says the well-travelled John Hays was the source, having been sent to England by Hussey to learn about them in 1847. Williams also notes that Captain Jennings had English experience with this technology.

[103] Cooper, "Historical Sketch of Smelting and Refining Lake Copper." p. 24.

[104] "History."

[105] "The Iron Bank Building," *Pittsburgh Post,* June 21 1859. p. 1.

[106] "Removal," *Pittsburgh Post,* September 9 1859. p. 2.

[107] "Pittsburgh Copper and Brass Rolling Mills," *Pittsburgh Post Gazette,* July 6 1881. p. 3.

[108] Heinz History Center (Detre Library & Archives 1876).

Endnotes for Steel

[109] J.S. Jeans, *Steel, Its History, Manufacture, and Uses* (London and New York: E & F Spon, 1880). p. 338.

[110] Marshall and Lamb Brain, Robert, "How Iron and Steel Work," https://science.howstuffworks.com/iron3.htm.

[111] Peter Temin, *Iron and Steel in 19th-century America* (Cambridge, MA: MIT Press, 1964). p. 125.

[112] Geoffrey Tweedale, *Sheffield Steel and America: A Century of Commercial and Technological Interdependence 1830-1930* (Cambridge, London, New York, New Rochelle: Cambridge University Press, 1987). p.47.

[113] "Crucible Industries," https://en.wikipedia.org/wiki/Crucible_Industries.

[114] Malcolm Keir, *Manufacturing - a Volume of Industries in America* (New York: The Ronald Press, 1928). p. 28.

[115] Jeans, *Steel, Its History, Manufacture, and Uses.* pp. 320ff.

[116] Ibid.

[117] Tweedale, *Sheffield Steel and America: A Century of Commercial and Technological Interdependence 1830-1930.* p. 1.

[118] Ibid. p. 5.

[119] Harrison Gilmer, "Birth of the American Crucible Steel Industry," *Western Pennsylvania Historical Magazine*, March 1953. pp 25-26.

[120] Tweedale, *Sheffield Steel and America: A Century of Commercial and Technological Interdependence 1830-1930.* p. 9.

[121] Ibid. pp. 13-14.

[122] James M. Swank, *The History of the Manufacture of Steel in All Ages* (Philadelphia: The American Iron and Steel Institute, 1892). p. 397.

[123] Tweedale, *Sheffield Steel and America: A Century of Commercial and Technological Interdependence 1830-1930.* p. 15, citing Swank.

[124] Gilmer, "Birth of the American Crucible Steel Industry." p. 24.

[125] Tweedale, *Sheffield Steel and America: A Century of Commercial and Technological Interdependence 1830-1930.* p. 16.

[126] Gilmer, "Birth of the American Crucible Steel Industry." p. 28.

[127] *In Memoriam Calvin Wells*, (Philadelphia: J.P. Lippincott Co., 1910). p. 25.

[128] *A Genealogical and Biographical History of Allegheny County, Pennsylvania.* p. 261.

[129] Ellis Paxson Oberholtzer, *Philadelphia - a History of the City and Its People a Record of 225 Years*, vol. IV (Philadelphia: S.J. Clark Publishing Company, 1912). p. 424.

[130] *In Memoriam Calvin Wells.* p.23

[131] Gilmer, "Birth of the American Crucible Steel Industry." p. 21.

[132] Ibid. p. 26.

[133] *Hussey, Wells & Co. Manufacturers of All Types of Cast Steel*, c.1870. Galaxy Publishing Co.

[134] G.M. Hopkins & Co., "Pittsburgh Ninth Ward Tenth Ward Plate 32," (Philadelphia: G.M. Hopkins, 1872).

[135] Tweedale, *Sheffield Steel and America: A Century of Commercial and*

Technological Interdependence 1830-1930. p. 24.

[136] Ibid. p. 26.

[137] *A Genealogical and Biographical History of Allegheny County, Pennsylvania.* p. 256.

[138] *Sheffield Steel and America: A Century of Commercial and Technological Interdependence 1830-1930.* p. 20.

[139] Gilmer, "Birth of the American Crucible Steel Industry." p. 17.

[140] Herbert N. Casson, *The Romance of Steel - the Story of a Thousand Millionaires* (New York: A.S. Barnes & Co., 1907). p.16.

[141] Swank, *The History of the Manufacture of Steel in All Ages.* p. 393.

[142] Tweedale, *Sheffield Steel and America: A Century of Commercial and Technological Interdependence 1830-1930.* p. 23.

[143] "Proofs of the Superiority of Hussey, Wells & Co's. American Cast Steel," ed. Wells & Co. Hussey (Pittsburgh: W.S. Haven, 1866). p.7, letter dated September 13, 1864.

[144] "Pittsburgh Cast-Steelworks," *Scientific American (1845-1908)* 1864. p. 263.

[145] Ibid.

[146] Mining Certificate, ed. No. 237 General Land Office (1872).

[147] "Hussey, Wells & Co.'S Steelworks," *Railway Times (1860-1872)*, May 30 1868. p. 171.

[148] Ibid.

[149] Ibid. p. 172.

[150] "R.G. Dun Credit Report Volumes 1840-95." p. 1.194.

[151] Ibid. p. 1.193.

[152] Ibid. p. 1.404

[153] "Hussey, Wells & Co.'S Steelworks." p. 171.

[154] Tweedale, *Sheffield Steel and America: A Century of Commercial and Technological Interdependence 1830-1930.* p. 188.

[155] Swank, *The History of the Manufacture of Steel in All Ages.* p. 394.

[156] Tweedale, *Sheffield Steel and America: A Century of Commercial and Technological Interdependence 1830-1930.*

[157] Willam W. Wiliams, "Thomas M. Howe," *Magazine of Western History*, October 1885. p. 551.

[158] "Dissolution," *Pittsburgh Daily Commercial*, November 22 1876. p. 1.

[159] Tweedale, *Sheffield Steel and America: A Century of Commercial and Technological Interdependence 1830-1930.* p. 26.

[160] "Industrial Notes," (Pittsburgh 1888). p. 5.

[161] "Crucible Industries."

[162] *A Genealogical and Biographical History of Allegheny County, Pennsylvania.* p. 256.

[163] Jeans, *Steel, Its History, Manufacture, and Uses.* p. 16.

[164] Casson, *The Romance of Steel - the Story of a Thousand Millionaires.* p. 11.

[165] LaVern W. Spring, "Non-Technical Chats on Iron and Steel," 1917. p. 10.

[166] Tweedale, *Sheffield Steel and America: A Century of Commercial and Technological Interdependence 1830-1930.* p. 27.

[167] Ibid. p. 188, citing American Iron and Steel Association *Annual Statistical Report*

(1905), p.107.

[168] Casson, *The Romance of Steel - the Story of a Thousand Millionaires.* pp. 6-10.

[169] Keir, *Manufacturing - a Volume of Industries in America.* pp. 186-188.

[170] *The Industrial Revolution in American: Iron and Steel,* (Santa Barbara: ABC CLIO Inc., 2005).

[171] Casson, *The Romance of Steel - the Story of a Thousand Millionaires.* p. 6.

[172] Ibid. p.11.

[173] Ibid. p. 17.

[174] James Howard Bridge, *The inside History of the Carnegie Steel Company* (Pittsburgh: University of Pittsburgh Press, 1991). pp. 150-151. Bridge mistakenly cites Hussey, Wells & Co. as a partner, but Hussey's steel company had been Hussey, Howe & Co. since 1876..

[175] Paul Krause, *The Battle for Homestead, 1880-1892: Politics, Culture, and Steel* (Pittsburgh: University of Pittsburgh Press, 1992). pp. 166-167.

[176] Ibid. pp. 167-168.

[177] Bridge, *The inside History of the Carnegie Steel Company.* p. 151.

[178] "Brevities," *Pittsburgh Post-Gazette*, January 29 1881. p. 4.

[179] Krause, *The Battle for Homestead, 1880-1892: Politics, Culture, and Steel.* p. 170.

[180] Bridge, *The inside History of the Carnegie Steel Company.* p. 151.

[181] Krause, *The Battle for Homestead, 1880-1892: Politics, Culture, and Steel.* p. 166. Bridge makes the same point, p. 161.

[182] Bridge, *The inside History of the Carnegie Steel Company.* pp. 154-159.

[183] Krause, *The Battle for Homestead, 1880-1892: Politics, Culture, and Steel.* p. 179.

[184] "The Iron and Steel Workers - Hussey, Howe & Co. Accede to the Terms of the Men," *New York Times*, May 23 1883. p.1.

[185] C.H. Odell, October 29 1883. The sixth, and smallest investor, with only a $20,000 share, Andrew Kloman, had died in 1881. Clark, although no longer superintendent, remained an investor with his $40,000 share. "Managers" is the term used in various documents for corporate directors.

[186] Burton J. Hendrick, "The Life of Andrew Carnegie," (New York: Hastings House, 1932). p. 301.

[187] "Labor Notes," *Pittsburgh Post-Gazette*, October 22 1883. p 2.

[188] Bridge, *The inside History of the Carnegie Steel Company.* Pp. 130ff, p. 169, p. 254

[189] Krause, *The Battle for Homestead, 1880-1892: Politics, Culture, and Steel.* pp. 51-52, 58-60.

[190] Ibid. pp. 62-63, footnote 18, quoting the *Vulcan Record,* January 1868, p.14.

[191] "Our Working Classes", *New York Times*, February 22 1869. p. 2.

[192] Krause, *The Battle for Homestead, 1880-1892: Politics, Culture, and Steel.* p. 153.

[193] Ibid. p. 98.

[194] Ibid. p. 100.

[195] Peter Krass, *Carnegie* (Hoboken: John Wiley & Sons, 2002). p. 179.

[196] Odell. (Odell 1883), letter to Carnegie.

[197] "Hussey, Howe & Co. Limited Articles of Association," ed. Pennsylvania Bureau of Corporations and Charitable Organizations (1882).

[198] "Prominent Business Man Dead," *Pittsburgh Daily Post*, October 24 1909. p. 1.

[199] "C. Curtis Hussey Obituary," *Pittsburgh Post-Gazette*, March 3 1884. p. 4.

[200] "Hussey, howe & Co. Limited Articles of Association," ed. Pennsylvania Bureau of Corporations and Charitable Organizations (1885).

[201] "Howe, Brown & Co. Limited Articles of Association," ed. Pennsylvania Bureau of Corporations and Charities (1888).

[202] "Traders Gossip," *Pittsburgh Press*, February 2 1918. p. 22.

Endnotes for Philanthropy

[203] https://walkershire.net/data11/ps05/ps05_100.html

[204] *C.G. Hussey Photograph*, 1882. Mt. Pleasant Historical Society - Hussey archives.

[205] Nina de Angeli Wall, "Art and Industry in Philadelphia: Origins of the Philadelphia School of Design for Women," *Pennsylvania Magazine of History and Biography*, July 1993. pp.177-199.

[206] Christina Britta Dwyer, "Nineteenth Century Regional Women Artists: The Pittsburgh School of Design for Women, 1865-1904" (Chatham College, 1989). pp. 14-15.

[207] Wall, "Art and Industry in Philadelphia: Origins of the Philadelphia School of Design for Women."

[208] Dwyer, "Nineteenth Century Regional Women Artists: The Pittsburgh School of Design for Women, 1865-1904". p. 59

[209] Ibid. p. 46

[210] Ibid. p. 49

[211] Ibid. p. 58

[212] Ibid. p. 70

[213] "School of Design for Women," *Pittsburgh Dail Commercial*, January 23 1874. p. 4

[214] "Clever Art Work of Women Is Shown," *Pittsburgh Weekly Gazette*, February 3 1903. p.6

[215] "1878 Pittsburgh School of Design for Women Ms60 Uncertified."

[216] "Nineteenth Century Regional Women Artists: The Pittsburgh School of Design for Women, 1865-1904". p. 64.

[217] Williams, "Curtis G. Hussey." p. 346.

[218] Dwyer, "Nineteenth Century Regional Women Artists: The Pittsburgh School of Design for Women, 1865-1904". pp. 141-144.

[219] Ibid. p. 200 footnote 4.

[220] Ibid. pp. 200-201.

[221] *Central Y.M.C.A. Building, 7th St. And Penn. Ave., Pittsburgh, Pa.*, pre-1915. I. Robbins & Son.

[222] "Nineteenth Century Regional Women Artists: The Pittsburgh School of Design for Women, 1865-1904". pp. 272-274.

[223] Ibid. p. 282.

[224] Ibid. p. 287.

[225] James Purdie Knowles, "Samuel A. Purdie, His Life and Letters, His Work as a

Missionary and Spanish Writer and Publisher in Mexico and Central America," (Plainfield, IN: Publishing Association of Friends, 1908). pp. 57ff.

226 William Buys, "Quakers in Indiana in the 19th-century" (University of Florida, 1973). p 126.; Mahalah Jay, "Historic Sketch of Friends Mission Work in Mexico, Tamualispas," in *Foreign Mission Work of American Friends* (American Friends Board of Foreign Missions, 1912). pp 1-2, 12.

227 "Quakers in Latin America: Friends Historical Collection Resources," Guildford College, http://library.guilford.edu/c.php?g=111809&p=723697.

228James Purdie Knowles, "Samuel A. Purdie," in *His life and letters, his work as a missionary and Spanish writer and publisher in Mexico and Central America* (Plainfield, IN: Publishing Association of Friends, 1908). pp. 155-156.

229 Jay, "Historic Sketch of Friends Mission Work in Mexico, Tamualispas." pp. 13-14.

230 Ibid. pp. 20-21

231 Knowles, "Samuel A. Purdie." p. 106

232 "Quakers in Latin America: Friends Historical Collection Resources."

233 Russell W. Irvine, "The African American Quest for Institutions of Higher Education before the Civil War," (Lewiston, NY: The Edmund Mellen Press, 2010). Citing "Acts of the General Assembly of the Commonwealth of PA, *Laws of Pennsylvania Session of 1849*, No. 194, March 20", p, 342, in footnote 12, page 395.

234 Ibid. p. 335.

235 Ibid. p. 343

236 Ibid. p. 342

237 "Avery College. Board of Trustees," *Christian Recorder*, November 14 1868.

238 Irvine, "The African American Quest for Institutions of Higher Education before the Civil War." p. 393.

239 Ibid. p. 385.

240 Ibid. p. 338.

241 Ibid. p. 341.

242 Ibid. p. 339, p. 383.

243 Ibid. p. 382.

244 Ibid. pp. 384-385.

245 Ibid. p. 387.

246 Ibid. fp. 344, footnote 18, p. 395 citing a letter from Douglass to John Peck, *the Black Abolitionist Papers,* Reel 6, frame-number 0365. Peck was one of the founding Avery College trustees.

247 Ibid. pp. 389-390.

248 Ibid. pp. 386-387.

249 Ibid. p. 390.

250 Bernard Morris, "Avery College - Symbol with Preserving." p.21

251 Ibid. p. 21

252 "Freedmen's Aid Commission of Western Pennsylvania, Eastern Ohio, and Western Virginia," *Pittsburgh Daily Commercial*, February 4 1865. p.2.

253 "Anniversary of the Freedmen's Aid Association," *Pittsburgh Gazette*, December 12, 1865. p. 4.

254 Louis W. Coban, "History of Allegheny Observatory," University of Pittsburgh,

http://www.pitt.edu/~aobsvtry/history.html.

[255] "Dedication of the New Allegheny Observatory," in *Miscellaneous Scientific Papers of the Allegheny Observatory* (Lancaster PA: New Era Printing Company, 1913). pp. 32-33.

[256] "Dedication of the New Allegheny Observatory." p. 34.

[257] Wallace R. Beardsley, "Samuel Pierpont Langley -- His Early Academics at the University of Western Pennsylvania" (University of Pittsburgh, 1978). pp. 18-19, citing a letter Thaw wrote to Howe and Hussey in which the said that the debt of $13,191 held by the three was "relinquished" Letter No. 1 in the Thaw collection at the Historical Society of Western Pa.

[258] John E. Parke, "Recollections of Seventy Years and Historical Gleanings of Allegheny City," (Boston: Rand, Avery and Co Franklin Press, 1886). p.181.

[259] "U.S., School Catalogs, 1765-1935," (Provo, UT: Ancestry.com Operations, Inc., 2012).

[260] Coban, "History of Allegheny Observatory."

[261] Gilmer, "Birth of the American Crucible Steel Industry." p. 29.

[262] Alberta Dysart, *Chatham College, the First 90 Years* (Pittsburgh PA: Chatham College, 1969). p. 257.

[263] Eli I. Hayes, *Pittsburgh Female College ... Pittsburgh, Pa,* 1877. Titus, Simmons, & Titus.

[264] *A Genealogical and Biographical History of Allegheny County, Pennsylvania.* p. 258.

[265] *Western Christian Advocate*, August 30 1882.

[266] C.G. Hussey, "Last Will and Testament," ed. Pennsylvania Probate Records (1889). Volumes 43-44, pp. 245-253.

[267] Ibid.

[268] "Colored Orphans' Home," *Pittsburgh Press*, December 27 1896. p. 7.

[269] G.M. Hopkins & Co., "Allegheny City Vol. 2 Plate 2," (Philadelphia: G.M. Hopkins, 1890).

[270] Parke, "Recollections of Seventy Years and Historical Gleanings of Allegheny City." p. 155. In 1871 Hussey made an uncharacteristically minor donation of $50 toward the $18,192 raised by the Pittsburgh and Allegheny Home for the Friendless to purchase additional land from Henry Forsyth.

[271] "To the Honorable the Select and Common Councils of the City of Allegheny," ed. Heinz History Center (Detre Library & Archives 1857).

[272] "Allegheny Commons," National Park Service, https://www.nps.gov/nr/feature/places/13000740.htm.

[273] Dysart, *Chatham College, the First 90 Years.* p.14.

[274] Hussey, "Last Will and Testament." p. 246.

[275] *A Genealogical and Biographical History of Allegheny County, Pennsylvania.* p. 258.

[276] Adelaide Mellier Nevin, "The Social Mirror - a Character Sketch of the Women of Pittsburgh and Vicinity During the First Century of the County's Existence. Society to-Day.," (Pittsburgh: T.W. Nevin, 1888). pp.81-82.

[277] Gilmer, "Birth of the American Crucible Steel Industry."; "Wentt-Pa-Misc- Records,"

AfriGeneas.com, http://www.afrigeneas.com/slavedata/Wentt-VA-PA- 1763.txt. The AfriGeneas source was Paul Redden's blog at http://users.inna.net/~redden, which is now defunct. Redden reported transcribing a text that he believes was a C.G. Hussey speech on an 1858 Georgia slave auction that he saw.

[278]*National Citizen and Ballot Box* 1881

[279] "The Funeral of C. Curtis Hussey," *Pittsburgh Post-Gazette.* p. 4.

[280] "Obituary Notes," *Pittsburgh Daily Post*, January 8 1877. p. 4.

[281] Williams, "Curtis G. Hussey." p. 343.

[282] "Pittsburgh (Steel) Historical Marker," http://explorepahistory.com/hmarker.php?markerId=1-A-23D.

[283] Beardsley, "Samuel Pierpont Langley -- His Early Academics at the University of Western Pennsylvania". pp. 24, 160, citing "unidentified newspaper clipping, Thaw Collection, archives Historical Society of Western PA, June 23, 1867

[284] Krause, *The Battle for Homestead, 1880-1892: Politics, Culture, and Steel.* pp 84-85.

[285] *A Genealogical and Biographical History of Allegheny County, Pennsylvania.* p. 257.

[286] "Pittsburgh Millionaires," *St. Louis Post-Dispatch*, November 5 1885. p. 7.

[287] "Dr. Hussey Dead," *Pittsburgh Post-Gazette*, April 26 1893. p. 2.

[288] "Dr. C. G. Hussey Dead," *Pittsburgh Dispatch*, April 26 1893. p. 6.

[289] Nevin, "The Social Mirror - a Character Sketch of the Women of Pittsburgh and Vicinity During the First Century of the County's Existence. Society to-Day.." pp.81- 82.

[290] Hussey, "Last Will and Testament."

[291]"Inventory and Appraisal Estate of C.G.Hussey Dec'd" Allegheny County Orphan Court (Pittsburgh 1893) In 10 521 383 and "Account of Edward B. Alsop, Et Al Extrs of the Estate of C.G. Hussey Deceased," ed. Allegheny County Orphan Court (Pittsburgh1898). Vol. 75, p. 478.

[292] "Hussey, howe & Co. Limited Articles of Association."; "Hussey, Howe & Co. Limited Articles of Association."; "Hussey, Howe & Co. Limited Articles of Association," ed. Pennsylvania Bureau and Corporations and Charitable Organizations (1880); "Howe, Brown & Co. Limited Articles of Associaton."(1888). The multiple filings of 1880, 1882, 1885, 1888 were necessary because the partnership filings stipulated two or three year terms. The filing of 1888 corresponds with the sale of the Hussey interest to Howe and Brown, indicating that Hussey chose expiration date of the 1885 limited partnership to sell.

[293] "Dr. C. G. Hussey Dead," *Boston Daily Globe*, April 26 1893.

[294] "More Fifth Avenue Protests," *Pittsburgh Dispatch*, February 4 1892. p. 9.

[295] Edward H. Hussey, February 4 1907. James Brown, May 7 1907.

[296] et al. Edward B. Alsop, to The Superior Trust Co, "Agreement and Declaration of Trust," (Houghton Michigan: Stone, Wieder, and Schulte, Attorneys and Counselors, 1916).

[297] William Veeser, 1978; William W. Gilkey, 1979.

Endnotes for Appendix (Other Hussey Enterprises)

298 Chaput, *The Cliff; America's First Great Copper Mine*. p.77.

299 Thurston, *Pittsburgh as It Is; or Facts and Figures Exhibiting the Past and Present of Pittsburgh, Its Advantages, Resources, Manufactures, and Commerce*. p.134.

References

"1878 Pittsburgh School of Design for Women Ms60 Uncertified."

A Genealogical and Biographical History of Allegheny County, Pennsylvania. Edited by Thomas Cushing. Baltimore, MD: Genealogical Publishing Co., 2007. History of Allegheny County, Penn. Part II, 1889.

"Account of Edward B. Alsop, Et Al Extrs of the Estate of C.G. Hussey Deceased." edited by Allegheny County Orphan Court, 478. Pittsburgh, 1898.

"Allegheny Commons." National Park Service, https://www.nps.gov/nr/feature/places/13000740.htm.

"Anniversary of the Freedmen's Aid Association." *Pittsburgh Gazette*, December 12, 1865, 4.

"Avery College. Board of Trustees." *Christian Recorder*, November 14 1868. Beardsley, Wallace R. "Samuel Pierpont Langley -- His Early Academics at the University of Western Pennsylvania." University of Pittsburgh, 1978.

Brain, Marshall and Lamb, Robert. "How Iron and Steel Work." https://science.howstuffworks.com/iron3.htm.

"Brevities." *Pittsburgh Post-Gazette*, January 29 1881, 4.

Bridge, James Howard. *The inside History of the Carnegie Steel Company.* Pittsburgh: University of Pittsburgh Press, 1991.

Brown, James. May 7 1907.

Buys, William. "Quakers in Indiana in the 19th-century." University of Florida, 1973. "C. Curtis Hussey Obituary." *Pittsburgh Post-Gazette*, March 3 1884, 4.

"C.G. Hussey." Signed C.G. Hussey. Philadelphia: Galaxy Pub. Co., 1860.

"C.G. Hussey Photograph." Mt. Pleasant Historical Society - Hussey archives, 1882. Carnegie, Andrew. "The Autobiography of Andrew Carnegie."

Casson, Herbert N. *The Romance of Steel - the Story of a Thousand Millionaires.* New York: A.S. Barnes & Co., 1907.

"Central Y.M.C.A. Building, 7th St. And Penn. Ave., Pittsburgh, Pa.". Pittsburgh PA: I. Robbins & Son, pre-1915.

Certificate, Mining. edited by No. 237 General Land Office, 1872.

Chaput, Donald. *The Cliff; America's First Great Copper Mine.* Kalamazoo, Michigan: Sequoia Press, 1971.

"Clever Art Work of Women Is Shown." *Pittsburgh Weekly Gazette*, February 3 1903. Co., G.M. Hopkins &. "Allegheny City Vol. 2 Plate 2." Philadelphia: G.M. Hopkins, 1890.

———. "Parts of Wards 13 & 14 Pittsburgh Plate 2." Philadelphia: G.M. Hopkins, 1882.

————. "Pittsburgh Ninth Ward Tenth Ward Plate 32." Philadelphia: G.M. Hopkins, 1872.

Coban, Louis W. "History of Allegheny Observatory." University of Pittsburgh, http://www.pitt.edu/~aobsvtry/history.html.

"Colored Orphans' Home." *Pittsburgh Press*, December 27 1896, 7.

Cooper, James B. "Historical Sketch of Smelting and Refining Lake Copper."

Proceedings of the Lake Superior Mining Institute, March 5-9 1901, 44-49 (23-24).

Counties of Morgan, Monroe and Brown, Indiana: Historical and Biographical. Chicago: F.A. Battery & Co., 1884.

"Crucible Industries." https://en.wikipedia.org/wiki/Crucible_Industries.

"Curtis Grubb Hussey." http://legdb.iga.in.gov/ - !/legislator/2172/Curtis-Hussey. "Dedication of the New Allegheny Observatory." In *Miscellaneous Scientific Papers of the Allegheny Observatory.* Lancaster PA: New Era Printing Company, 1913. "Dissolution." *Pittsburgh Daily Commercial*, November 22 1876.

"Dr. C. G. Hussey Dead." *Boston Daily Globe*, April 26 1893. "Dr. C. G. Hussey Dead." *Pittsburgh Dispatch*, April 26 1893. "Dr. Hussey Dead." *Pittsburgh Post-Gazette*, April 26 1893.

Dwyer, Christina Britta. "Nineteenth Century Regional Women Artists: The Pittsburgh School of Design for Women, 1865-1904." Chatham College, 1989.

Dysart, Alberta. *Chatham College, the First 90 Years.* Pittsburgh PA: Chatham College, 1969.

Edward B. Alsop, et al., to The Superior Trust Co. "Agreement and Declaration of Trust." Houghton Michigan: Stone, Wieder, and Schulte, Attorneys and Counselors, 1916.

Egleston, Thomas. "Copper Refining in the United States." *Transactions of the American Institute of Mining Engineers May, 1880 to September, 1881*, 1881.

Foster, J.. W. ; Whitney, J. D. *Report on the Geology and Topography of a portion of the Lake Superior Land District, in the State of Michigan ; ... in two parts. Part I. Copper Lands.*

Washington: Printed for the House of Reps. 1850.

"Freedmen's Aid Commission of Western Pennsylvania, Eastern Ohio, and Western Virginia." *Pittsburgh Daily Commercial*, February 4 1865.

Gates, William B. Jr. *Michigan Copper and Boston Dollars an Economic History of the Michigan Copper Mining Industry.* Cambridge, MA: Harvard University Press, 1951.

Gilkey, William W. 1979.

Gilmer, Harrison. "Birth of the American Crucible Steel Industry." *Western Pennsylvania Historical Magazine*, March 1953.

"Great Lakes Area Map." Google Maps.

Hayes, Eli I. "Pittsburgh Female College ... Pittsburgh, Pa." Philadelphia: Titus, Simmons, & Titus, 1877.

Hendrick, Burton J. "The Life of Andrew Carnegie." New York: Hastings House, 1932. "History." http://www.husseycopper.com/about/history/.

History of the Upper Peninsula of Michigan: Containing a Full Account of Its Early Settlement, Its Growth, Development, and Resources, an Extended Description of Its Iron and Copper Mines. Chicago: Western Historical Co., A.T. Andreas Proprietor, 1883.

"Howe, Brown & Co. Limited Articles of Association." edited by Pennsylvania Bureau of Corporations and Charities, 1888.

Hussey, A. H. In *Hussey Archives*: Mt. Pleasant Historical Society, 1865.

Hussey, C.G. "Last Will and Testament." edited by Pennsylvania Probate Records, 245-53, 1889.

Hussey, Edward H. February 4 1907.

"Hussey, Howe & Co. Limited Articles of Association." edited by Pennsylvania Bureau of Corporations and Charitable Organizations, 1882.

"Hussey, Howe & Co. Limited Articles of Association." edited by Pennsylvania Bureau and Corporations and Charitable Organizations, 1880.

"Hussey, Wells & Co. Manufacturers of All Types of Cast Steel." Philadelphia: Galaxy Publishing Co., c.1870.

"Hussey, Wells & Co.'S Steelworks." *Railway Times (1860-1872)*, May 30 1868, 171. "Hussey, howe & Co. Limited Articles of Association." edited by Pennsylvania Bureau of Corporations and Charitable Organizations, 203-17, 1885.

Hyde, Charles K. *Copper for America: The United States Copper Industry from Colonial Times to the 1990s.* Tuscon: University of Arizona Press, 1998.

In Memoriam Calvin Wells. Philadelphia: J.P. Lippincott Co., 1910.

"Indiana Yearly Meeting minutes, 1823-1833. http://search.ancestry.com/cgi-bin/sse.dll?indiv=try&db=QuakerMeetMins&h=1155653

"Industrial Notes." 5. Pittsburgh, 1888.

Irvine, Russell W. "The African American Quest for Institutions of Higher Education before the Civil War." Lewiston, NY: The Edmund Mellen Press, 2010.

Jay, Mahalah. "Historic Sketch of Friends Mission Work in Mexico, Tamualispas." In *Foreign Mission Work of American Friends*: American Friends Board of Foreign Missions, 1912.

Jeans, J.S. *Steel, Its History, Manufacture, and Uses.* London and New York: E & F Spon, 1880.

Keir, Malcolm. *Manufacturing - a Volume of Industries in America.* New York: The Ronald Press, 1928.

Knowles, James Purdie. "Samuel A. Purdie." In *His life and letters, his work as a missionary and Spanish writer and publisher in Mexico and Central America.* Plainfield, IN: Publishing Association of Friends, 1908.

———. "Samuel A. Purdie, His Life and Letters, His Work as a Missionary and Spanish Writer and Publisher in Mexico and Central America." Plainfield, IN: Publishing Association of Friends, 1908.

Krass, Peter. *Carnegie.* Hoboken: John Wiley & Sons, 2002.

Krause, Paul. *The Battle for Homestead, 1880-1892: Politics, Culture, and Steel.* Pittsburgh: University of Pittsburgh Press, 1992.

"Labor Notes." *Pittsburgh Post-Gazette*, October 22 1883, 2.

"More Fifth Avenue Protests." *Pittsburgh Dispatch*, February 4 1892.

"Morgan County, Indiana." Wikipedia, https://en.wikipedia.org/wiki/Morgan_County,_Indiana.

Morris, Bernard. "Avery College - Symbol with Preserving."

Murdoch, Angus. *Boom Copper the Story of the First U.S. Mining Boom.* New York: The MacMillan Company, 1945.

National Citizen and Ballot Box, 1881.

Nevin, Adelaide Mellier. "The Social Mirror - a Character Sketch of the Women of Pittsburgh and Vicinity During the First Century of the County's Existence. Society to-Day.". Pittsburgh: T.W. Nevin, 1888.

Oberholtzer, Ellis Paxson. *Philadelphia - a History of the City and Its People a Record of 225 Years.* Vol. IV, Philadelphia: S.J. Clark Publishing Company, 1912.

"Obituary Notes." *Pittsburgh Daily Post*, January 8 1877. Odell, C.H. October 29 1883.

"Our Working Classes" *New York Times*, February 22 1869.

Parke, John E. "Recollections of Seventy Years and Historical Gleanings of Allegheny City." Boston: Rand, Avery and Co Franklin Press, 1886.

The Pennocks of Primitive Hall, http://www.pennock.ws/surnames/nti/nti11407.html "Notes for Jonathan Binns."

Pettengill, Robert B. "The United States Foreign Trade in Copper 1790-1932."

American Economic Review XXV (1935): 426-41. "Pittsburgh (Steel) Historical Marker."

http://explorepahistory.com/hmarker.php?markerId=1-A-23D. "Pittsburgh Cast-Steelworks." *Scientific American (1845-1908)*, 1864, 263. "Pittsburgh Copper and Brass Rolling Mills." *Pittsburgh Post Gazette*, July 6 1881. "Pittsburgh Millionaires." *St. Louis Post-Dispatch*, November 5 1885.

"Prominent Business Man Dead." *Pittsburgh Daily Post*, October 24 1909.

"Proofs of the Superiority of Hussey, Wells & Co's. American Cast Steel." edited by Wells & Co. Hussey. Pittsburgh: W.S. Haven, 1866.

Purn, Donald V. "Great Copper Rush in Upper Michigan 1842." http://www.oldalgonquin.net/Schooner/copperrush.html.

"Quakers in Latin America: Friends Historical Collection Resources." Guildford College, http://library.guilford.edu/c.php?g=111809&p=723697.

"R.G. Dun Credit Report Volumes 1840-95." "Removal." *Pittsburgh Post*, September 9 1859.

Reynolds, Terry S. "Curtis Grubb Hussey, Smelting/Refining Industry Leaders, Copper Industry Leaders, Meatpackers." American National Biography Online.

Ryan, Daniel J. *History of Ohio: The Rise and Progress of an American State.* Vol. 4, New York1912.

"School of Design for Women." *Pittsburgh Dail Commercial*, January 23 1874.

"Ship Canal at Sault St. Marie." *Pittsburgh Daily Post*, January 8 1852, 3.

Shriver, Phillip R., and Jr. Wunderlin, Clarence E. *The Documentary Heritage of Ohio*. Athens, Ohio: Ohio University Press, 2000.

"Soo Locks." https://en.wikipedia.org/wiki/Soo_Locks.

Spring, LaVern W. "Non-Technical Chats on Iron and Steel." 1917.

Swank, James M. *The History of the Manufacture of Steel in All Ages*. Philadelphia: The American Iron and Steel Institute, 1892.

Temin, Peter. *Iron and Steel in 19th-century America*. Cambridge, MA: MIT Press, 1964.

Tenney, William J, ed. *Mining Magazine*, 1855.

"The Funeral of C. Curtis Hussey." *Pittsburgh Post-Gazette*.

The Industrial Revolution in American: Iron and Steel. Santa Barbara: ABC CLIO Inc., 2005.

"The Iron and Steel Workers - Hussey, Howe & Co. Accede to the Terms of the Men." *New York Times*, May 23 1883.

"The Iron Bank Building." *Pittsburgh Post*, June 21 1859, 1.

Thurston, George H. *Pittsburgh as It Is; or Facts and Figures Exhibiting the Past and Present of Pittsburgh, Its Advantages, Resources, Manufactures, and Commerce*. Pittsburgh: W.S. Haven, 1857.

"To the Honorable the Select and Common Councils of the City of Allegheny." edited by Heinz History Center: Detre Library & Archives

"To the Honorable the Select and Common Councils of the City of Allegheny", 1857. "Traders Gossip." *Pittsburgh Press*, February 2 1918, 22.

Tweedale, Geoffrey. *Sheffield Steel and America: A Century of Commercial and Technological Interdependence 1830-1930*. Cambridge, London, New York, New Rochelle: Cambridge University Press, 1987.

"U.S., School Catalogs, 1765-1935." Provo, UT: Ancestry.com Operations, Inc., 2012. Veeser, William. 1978.

"Village of Mt. Pleasant." National Park Service, https://www.nps.gov/nr/travel/underground/oh4.htm.

Wall, Nina de Angeli. "Art and Industry in Philadelphia: Origins of the Philadelphia School of Design for Women." *Pennsylvania Magazine of History and Biography*, July 1993, 177-99.

"Wentt-Pa-Misc-Records." AfriGeneas.com, http://www.afrigeneas.com/slavedata/Wentt-VA-PA-1763.txt.

Western Christian Advocate, August 30 1882.

Wiliams, Willam W. "Thomas M. Howe." *Magazine of Western History*, October 1885, 550-56.

Williams, Ralph D. *The Honorable Peter White.* Cleveland Ohio: The Penton Publishing Co., 1907.

Williams, William W., ed. "Curtis G. Hussey." *Magazine of Western History*, 1886.

Acknowledgements

Thanks to the many people and institutions who supplied parts of the puzzle of Curtis Grubb Hussey, including:

Duncan Rea Wiliams, in whose genealogical blog I first encountered the short 1886 *Magazine of Western History* biography of C.G. Hussey that set me on the path that led to this book.

Anna Otto and Angela Feenerty, of Mt. Pleasant, Ohio, C.G. Hussey's hometown, who shared their knowledge of Hussey, his relatives, and the rich history of the local anti-slavery movement, as well as documents related to Hussey in the collections of the Mt. Pleasant Historical Society.

R. Grinnell of the University of Pittsburgh, who guided me in exploring the history of Avery College as well as setting me on the path to understanding the complexities of the ante-bellum anti-slavery movements.

Christopher T. Baer of the Hagley Museum and Library, who offered invaluable advice on how to research 19th-century corporate records.

Christina Britta Dwyer, whose unpublished Phd. dissertation at Chatham University provides the full history of the Pittsburgh School of Design for Women.

Staff at the Detre Library at the Heinz Center in Pittsburgh, who provided access to the Hussey documents in their possession, in particular an elegant lithograph of his steelworks at its height and to records related to the formation of the Allegheny Commons.

The Harvard Business School Library, for access to the R.G Dun records relating to Hussey's credit ratings, and to the Harvard Library system as a whole for access to the Hollis system through which I had access to many newspaper and magazine articles about Hussey not available elsewhere.

The newspapers.com website, for access to vast numbers of Hussey-related news articles and advertisements.

Family and friends who graciously read and commented on this manuscript.

www.ingramcontent.com/pod-product-compliance
Lightning Source LLC
Chambersburg PA
CBHW052343210326
41597CB00037B/6238